CALM SUTRA

A Guide to the Art and Science of Calm

By T Light

The Kama Sutra explores the sensual art of connection with another.

Calm Sutra explores the sensory art of connection with yourself.

This book is intended for informational and reflective purposes only. It is not a substitute for professional medical, psychological, or therapeutic advice. The author and publisher disclaim any liability arising directly or indirectly from the use of this material.

ISBN (paperback): 978-81-995778-0-0

Published by
The Crackajack Company

For the earlier version of me who lived
with anxiety and doubt,
and learned her way to calm.

TABLE OF CONTENTS

INTRODUCTION

The Kama Sutra explores the sensual art of connection with another.

Calm Sutra explores the sensory art of connection with yourself.

Let's start where it all began. At the start of life itself. Your brain is ancient, shaped by evolution, ruled by survival, and driven by habit. It repeats what feels familiar, even when it hurts.

But calm isn't a mystery; it's a trainable state.

Through neuroscience and simple daily practices, Calm Sutra teaches you how to rewire your nervous system, soothe the body's alarms, and turn stillness into strength.

You'll learn how language shapes emotion, how breath rewires thought, and how calm becomes a learned reflex.

Because serenity, like love, is mastered through attention, repetition, and touch.

This is Calm Sutra , a guide to the art and science of calm. I'm T-Light and together we will explore the space between biology and being, where calm isn't something you chase; it's something you can learn to become.

PART I: THE WIRING

WHEN THE WIRING SPARKS: HOW THE MIND SHORT-CIRCUITS ITSELF

CHAPTER 1

Let's start where it all starts ... in childhood.

or that one relationship that rewired the way we see ourselves, or that single moment that made us feel smaller than we ever were.

One rejection, one failure, one voice that said you're not enough, and our brain believed it.

Most of us did not break our own hearts ... or our own minds on purpose. Someone or something did the first damage long before we even knew what wiring was.

The Original Wound

Here is something they don't tell you in school. Between ages zero and seven, your brain is basically a sponge soaked in superglue. Everything sticks and I mean everything.

A child's brain operates primarily in theta wave state. The same brainwave pattern adults only reach during deep meditation or hypnosis. It's a state of pure absorption, no filters, no critical thinking, just download, download, download.

This is why a parent's offhand comment "Why can't you be more like your sister?" can echo in your head thirty years later.

Or why that teacher who called you lazy in third grade somehow becomes your inner voice during every job interview.

The Science Behind the Scar

Neuroscientist Dr. Bruce Lipton discovered that until age seven, children are essentially in a hypnotic state, directly downloading behaviors and beliefs into their subconscious mind. No quality control, no fact-checking.

These downloads become the unconscious programs that run 95% of your adult life.

Think about that.

Ninety-five percent of your daily thoughts, emotions, and behaviors are controlled by programs installed before you could spell your own name.

A 2019 study at Harvard found that adults who experienced emotional neglect in childhood showed measurably smaller hippocampi: the brain region responsible for memory and emotional regulation.

Smaller doesn't mean broken, but it does mean the alarm system got calibrated wrong.

Set to scream at shadows.

Maybe it began when you learned that love had conditions.

Be quiet ... be perfect ... don't upset anyone.

Children are programmed to please; elders aren't always programmed to protect.

Maybe it started with that one relationship that made you feel small.

Or the job interview you blew, after weeks of hope. Or the failure that rewrote your confidence in permanent red marker.

One bad story can carve a deep groove in the nervous system.

And the brain desperate for safety keeps replaying it like a scratched record.

The Neural Groove

Neuroscientists call this a "neural pathway,"

but I prefer to think of it as a dirt road in your brain. The first time something happens, the road is faint barely visible. But if a truck drives down that same path again and again: the path of rejection, failure, humiliation...Eventually, you've got a six-lane highway.

The brain, efficient as it is, will always choose the familiar highway over cutting through new dense forest terrain. Even if the familiar highway leads straight to panic.

That's how f**k-ups becomes a pattern. And you start living as if every next thing will collapse the same way.

The biology of "Never Again"

Here's what actually happens in your brain when something goes wrong.

Your amygdala, that almond-shaped alarm bell deep in your temporal lobe tags the experience with a massive emotional charge.

It basically spray-paints DANGER all over that memory in fluorescent red.

From that moment on, anything that even remotely resembles that situation triggers the same alarm.

Got rejected by your first love while you were wearing a blue sweater?

Your brain might now feel vaguely anxious around anything blue.

Sounds ridiculous, doesn't it?

But it's not. Because the amygdala doesn't do nuance, it does familiarity, it does survival.

Dr. Joseph LeDoux, a neuroscientist at NYU, discovered that the amygdala receives sensory information milliseconds before the thinking brain does.

That means your body is already flooding with cortisol and adrenaline before you even consciously register what is happening.

You're not overreacting. You're just getting information late to a party your body already started.

But Here is the Truth. The brain is plastic not prophetic.

The word plastic doesn't come from modern materials at all as we understand it in today's world. It comes from the Greek plastikos, from plassein, meaning to mold or shape.

So in neuroscience when we say the brain is plastic, we mean it is changeable, moldable, and capable of rewiring itself over time. Our brain can do that across an entire lifetime.

That process is called neuroplasticity: the brain's ability to create new connections and override old ones.

We'll dive deeper into it later. How habits reshape neural maps. How emotion tags can be rewritten. How deliberate thought literally sculpts gray matter For now, just know this. One disaster doesn't doom the rest of your life. It only programs a reflex and reflexes can be rewritten.

The Proof

A groundbreaking 2018 study at King's College London tracked adults who had experienced severe childhood trauma.

After just eight weeks of targeted therapy combined with mindfulness practice, brain scans showed measurable changes in their amygdala activity.

The alarm was still there but it wasn't screaming at everything anymore. It had learned to whisper.

Another study from Stanford found that neuroplasticity doesn't decline with age the way we thought. A seventy-year-old brain can form new neural connections just as effectively as a twenty-year-old's. It just needs more repetition, more time walking that new dirt road until it becomes the highway.

THE TIGER IN THE ROOM

To understand how and where this reflex began, we must travel far back, roughly two hundred thousand years, when the human brain was negotiating survival in jungles and forests amidst wild predatory animals, not inboxes and newsfeeds.

Back then, danger was immediate.

It was the rustle in the grass, not an unread message. The snap of a twig, not a notification.

The tiger was real, orange, striped, patient, waiting to kill.

Our ancestors' amygdala, the brain's alarm system, evolved to detect the faintest hint of threat. A flash of movement. A sound out of place. Adrenaline surged. Muscles tightened.

Cortisol flooded the bloodstream.

Fight.

Flee.

Freeze.

Anything to stay alive.

That system worked perfectly for our ancestors living in the jungles along with their fellow animals. It was the law of nature. If you heard a rustle and ran, you lived to reproduce, If you heard a rustle and thought, hmm, let me analyze this rationally, you became the tiger's lunch. Burp!

Natural selection did not favor the philosophical types. It favored the paranoid.

Fast-Forward to Now

The tigers are gone; we do not live in the jungles with wild animals anymore. But your amygdala never got the memo. It still scans for danger constantly, twenty-four seven.

And now the tiger wears new disguises.

The tiger is the email from your boss that says Can we talk?

The tiger is the silence after you send a message you shouldn't have. It's the look on someone's face that reminds you of rejection.

It's the bill you can't pay, the body you compare with the supermodels on Instagram, the feeling of being unseen in a world where likes mean validity.

To the primitive brain there is no difference between the growl in the jungle and the judgment in a room. Both mean unsafe. And so, it triggers the same cascade: heart racing, breath shortening, muscles stiffening, logic fading...

The numbers don't lie.

According to the American Psychological

Association, 77% of people regularly experience physical symptoms of stress. Not actual physical danger, just the thought of danger. The possibility of danger. The memory of danger.

Your body is spending energy fighting threats that exist only in your mind.

A 2020 study published in Nature Neuroscience found that chronic stress shrinks the prefrontal cortex. The part of your brain responsible for decision-making and self-control while simultaneously enlarging the amygdala.

Translation: The more stressed you are, the smaller your adult brain gets and the louder your toddler brain becomes. The toddler brain refers to our most primitive survival circuitry, sometimes called the primitive brain, and often described metaphorically as the "reptilian brain." These are the oldest neural systems, designed for survival, not reasoning.

You are not weak. Your brain has just slipped back to its primitive state. Fight, flight, or freeze.

Every time you felt unsafe as a child, every time affection was withheld, or approval dangled like bait, your nervous system recorded that as a potential tiger.

So now decades later when you face criticism or uncertainty, the body reacts as if claws are coming.

That's the sympathetic nervous system doing its job: mobilizing energy to protect you.

But in modern life the danger isn't physical, it's psychological and fighting or fleeing doesn't fix it.

That's why you spiral, because the old software of your primitive reptilian brain is trying to run a new world with old outdated rules.

The Ancient-Modern Mismatch

Anthropologists call this the "evolutionary mismatch theory."

Our bodies and brains evolved over millions of years to handle acute, physical threats.

Things that would either kill you immediately or let you live to reproduce.

But modern stressors are chronic, they never really go away. Job insecurity, relationship drama, financial pressure, existential dread, the news cycle, social comparison.

Your stress response system was designed for sprints, not marathons. And we've been making it run a marathon: uphill, in uncomfortable shoes, for decades.

Dr. Robert Sapolsky, a Stanford neuroendocrinologist (and my personal hero), put it perfectly in his book Why Zebras Don't Get Ulcers: "If you're a zebra running from a lion, your stress response is lifesaving.

If you're a human worried about your mortgage for thirty years, your stress response is slowly killing you."

Zebras don't get stress-related diseases.

Because once the lion gives up, the zebra's nervous system resets to calm within minutes. They literally shake it off and go back to grazing.

Humans? We replay the lion chase in our heads for years.

The lion isn't even real anymore, but we're still running...

THE OVERRIDE CODE

Here's where neuroscience gets hopeful.

The prefrontal cortex, the logical, forward- thinking part of your brain, has the authority to calm the primitive system.

It can override the alarm and whisper We're not being hunted ... we're just uncomfortable.

Slow breathing, grounded feet, naming what you feel, these are biological override codes.

Each slow exhale sends a message through the vagus nerve to the amygdala: false alarm.

When that message lands: cortisol drops, clarity returns, and you re-enter the present moment.

The Vagus Nerve: Your Body's Hotline to Calm Think of the vagus nerve as a telephone wire running from your brain to your heart, lungs, and gut. It's part of the parasympathetic nervous system, your rest-and-digest mode.

The vagus nerve is 90% afferent- meaning 90% of its fibers carry information from your body to your brain. Only 10% goes the other way i.e. from your brain to your body.

(Afferent nerves carry information from the body to the brain; efferent nerves carry commands from the brain to the body.)

Translation: Your body has more influence over your brain than your brain has over your body.

So, when you take a slow, deep breath- when you soften your shoulders, when you place your hand on your heart- You're not just "calming down" in some vague, woo-woo way.

You're sending a direct telegram to your amygdala that says, Stand down. No tigers here.

A 2017 study in Frontiers in Psychology found that just five minutes of slow breathing, inhaling for four counts, exhaling for six, decreased cortisol levels by an average of 23%.

That's not meditation. That's not years of practice. That's five minutes of deliberately lying to your body until it believes you.

That's how healing works. Not by erasing the tiger, but by teaching your body that most tigers are old memories now, with no power over the present you.

THE COMFORT OF CHAOS

And here is something deeper. The brain clings to the familiar , even when the familiar hurts.

A child raised around chaos will grow into an adult who mistakes calm for boredom, and conflict for love.

A daughter of a controlling father may find comfort in a controlling partner because her amygdala recognizes that rhythm.

To the survival brain - familiar equals safe-even when it's toxic.

The Neuroscience of Repetition Compulsion

Sigmund Freud called it "repetition compulsion" , the uncanny tendency to recreate painful patterns. He thought it was psychological. Turns out, it's neurological.

Dr. Bessel van der Kolk, trauma expert and author of The Body Keeps the Score, explains it this way: "The brain is a pattern-recognition machine. It constantly scans the environment looking for what's familiar so it can predict what happens next. Even if 'familiar' is painful, at least it's predictable , and to the nervous system, predictability equals safety."

A landmark study from UCLA found that people with chaotic childhoods showed heightened dopamine responses to unpredictability. Their brains literally got a pleasure hit from drama. Not because they enjoyed suffering. But because chaos felt like home. Familiar.

That's why we repeat old stories, choose the same kind of heartbreak in new faces, sabotage success just when it starts to feel good.

The nervous system isn't sabotaging you , it's trying to protect you from the shock of newness.

The Danger of Safety

I know this sounds backwards, but stay with me.

When you've been in survival mode for years, when hypervigilance is your baseline, actual peace can feel terrifying.

Because if you relax, who's watching for danger? If you let your guard down, when will the other shoe drop? If things are going well, how long until it all falls apart?

Dr. Stephen Porges, who developed Polyvagal Theory, calls this "neuroception" , the unconscious scanning for safety or threat. For some people, their neuroception is so finely tuned to danger that safety itself registers as suspicious.

Like a soldier returning from war who can't sleep without keeping one eye open.

Or a child of alcoholics who feels more anxious during the quiet moments than the loud ones.

One of my friends once said to me: "I don't trust the calm. Calm is just the time before everything goes to shit again."

And I said: "I know. But that's not wisdom.

That's just your nervous system's old software running."

Because growth is newness , and safety without growth becomes a cage.

Reclaiming your mind means teaching it that unfamiliar can also mean safe , that calm can be trusted „ that peace won't vanish the moment you stop bracing for pain.

THE PROGRAMMING OF PAIN

Think of it this way , your brain isn't broken.

It's just cautious to a fault.

It assumes that if something hurt once it might hurt forever.

But that's not prophecy , it's pattern recognition gone rogue.

Let me tell you about pain memory.

Scientists at Northwestern University

discovered something fascinating: After an injury heals, the brain often keeps a memory of the pain. Not the actual sensation, but the expectation of it.

People who've had chronic back pain, for instance, will often continue feeling pain years after the physical problem has resolved. The neurons that fired together during the injury have wired together into a pain network. And now they fire automatically, whether there's a reason or not.

The same thing happens with emotional pain.

Got your heart broken once? Your brain remembers. And now, even in a healthy relationship, it might keep signaling danger.

Not because something's wrong. But because it's remembering when something was.

The Default Setting

Neuroscientists have identified something called the Default Mode Network (DMN).

It's the brain's screensaver , what it does when it's not focused on a specific task.

For most people, the DMN is where rumination happens. Where you replay past failures. Where you rehearse future disasters.

Where you tell yourself stories about who you are and why things never work out.

A 2021 study from Yale found that people with anxiety and depression show hyperactivity in the DMN. Their brains literally can't stop thinking about problems.

Real or imagined.

But here's the good news: Meditation, breathwork, and even simple present- moment awareness have been shown to quiet the DMN. To take the brain offline from its default setting of worry to one of calm. You can change your screensaver.

RECLAIMING YOUR MIND

Reclaiming your mind begins with one new rule , not every echo of the past deserves a panic response.

That's what this book is about: understanding the hardware, debugging the code, and learning to operate from the part of your brain built for creation , not defense.

Before we go deeper into dopamine, cortisol, and the circuits of sabotage , remember this first principle.

You are not the sum of what went wrong.

You are the system learning to right itself.

The Three Keys to Rewiring

1. Awareness ,, You can't change what you don't notice 2. Repetition ,, The brain learns by frequency, not intensity 3. Safety ,, New patterns only stick when your nervous system feels safe enough to learn Think of yourself as both the student and the teacher. The ancient brain is the student , reactive, cautious, loyal to old lessons. The thinking brain is the teacher , patient, consistent, willing to show up every day with the same message until it finally lands.

You're not fighting yourself , You're teaching yourself.

And the beautiful thing about teaching?

Eventually, the lesson sticks. Eventually, calm becomes the new familiar. Eventually, your brain stops waiting for the tiger that's never coming.

Welcome to Calm Sutra.

Let's begin the repair.

PAUSE & PRACTICE: The First Five Minutes Before you move to the next chapter, try this.

Find a quiet space. Sit or stand comfortably.

Close your eyes if that feels safe, or soften your gaze downward.

Take five slow breaths.

Inhale through your nose for a count of four.

Hold gently for two.

Exhale through your mouth for six.

After the fifth breath, place one hand on your heart.

Feel the rhythm.

Feel the warmth.

Say quietly, out loud or in your mind: "I am safe right now."

You don't have to believe it yet. Just say it , Let your body hear it.

That's your first message to the amygdala.

The first new line of code.

Do this once a day , The brain is listening.

In the next chapter, we'll meet the family inside your head ,, the child, the parent, and the boss ,, and learn how to keep the right one in charge.

CHAPTER 2

THE MIND'S TRAPS: MEETING THE FAMILY IN YOUR HEAD

Your brain is loyal. Fiercely loyal. It believes whatever you tell it , and it defends that belief like a guard dog.

It's also ancient. A masterpiece that hasn't updated its software for millions of years.

It still runs on rules written when survival meant don't get eaten.

When human beings lived in wild jungles along with the tigers and bears, and every noise made them run into caves so they didn't get eaten.

That's why this brain, the primitive one, treats every unknown, everything unfamiliar as danger.

THE FAMILY MEETING

Let me try and explain this a bit better.

Imagine your brain as a house with three occupants. They've been living together for millennia. They don't always get along.

But they're stuck with each other.

At the base of your skull lives the reptilian brain , about 500 million years old.

It's the jungle brain , the I can spot the tiger brain.

You might wonder what use something that old still has. We've evolved and moved into cities and luxurious homes. Tigers are only in zoos and sanctuaries now.

So why is this reptilian brain still around?

But hey, let's not knock it. It's how God made it. It's this very reptilian brain that's keeping you alive right now.

The Reptilian Brain: The Child The reptilian brain controls digestion, sleep, body temperature, heartbeat, even the muscles that help you blink and breathe.

It manages your organs, your appetite, your bathroom breaks , everything your conscious mind doesn't have to micromanage.

So don't mock it. You need that ancient circuitry. It's the backstage crew running the show while you live your life under the stage lights.

But here's the thing.

The reptilian brain also runs on four fundamental programs: 1. Feeding , Am I hungry? Is that food?

Should I eat it?

2. Fighting , Is that a threat? Should I attack?

3. Fleeing , Can I escape? Where's the exit?

4. F*ing** , Can I reproduce with that?

(Yes, neuroscientists actually call these the "Four Fs" , science has a sense of humor after all)

This part of your brain doesn't think.

It reacts!

It's impulsive, binary, ruled by instinct.

Everything is either safe or dangerous.

Friend or food , Threat or opportunity.

No nuance. No context. No chill.

Dr. Paul MacLean, who developed the Triune Brain Model in the 1960s, described the reptilian brain as “fundamentally concerned with survival and reproduction”.

It doesn’t care about your career goals.

It doesn’t care about your emotional growth.

It cares about keeping you alive long enough to pass on your genes.

And it will hijack your entire system to do it.

A 2016 study at MIT found that when the brainstem (reptilian brain) detects a threat, it can override conscious decision-making in less than 200 milliseconds.

You don’t even know you’ve been hijacked until your heart is already racing.

That’s the child in your head.

Reactive, primal, terrified of the unknown.

THE LIMBIC SYSTEM: THE PARENT

Above the reptilian brain sits the limbic system, often called the emotional brain , roughly 200 million years old.

It gave mammals love, memory, belonging etc etc.

It keeps score by feeling, not logic.

This is where your emotions live.

Joy, grief, rage, affection, jealousy, nostalgia.

All the messy, beautiful, complicated stuff that makes you - you!

The limbic system includes several key structures: The Hippocampus , Your memory keeper.

It files experiences and decides what’s worth remembering.

A 2018 study from UC Irvine found that emotionally charged events get stamped with a "priority" tag. That's why you remember exactly where you were during your first kiss, but not what you had for lunch last Tuesday.

The Amygdala , Your smoke detector.

We met it in Chapter 1.

It's constantly scanning for danger and tagging memories with emotional significance. High-activation amygdala = high emotional memory.

Which is why trauma memories are so vivid, so visceral.

The Hypothalamus , Your thermostat.

It regulates hunger, thirst, sleep, sex drive, and stress hormones.

When you're stressed, it signals the adrenal glands to release cortisol.

When you're relaxed, it tells them to stand down.

The Nucleus Accumbens , Your reward center. The pleasure button.

Dopamine floods here when you eat chocolate, fall in love, or get a like on Instagram. This is also where addiction takes root.

When emotional safety feels threatened, the limbic system takes control , flooding the system with protective reactions.

It's here that attachment, desire, and even addiction is born , the emotional circuits that try to soothe what feels unsafe.

The Parent's Job: Protection Through Emotion The limbic system is the parent in your head.

Protective, reactive, feelings-first.

When you were a child and your actual parents comforted you, fed you, held you , your limbic system was taking notes.

It learned what love looks like. What safety feels like. What belonging sounds like.

Neuroscientist Dr. Allan Schore calls this “affect regulation” The capacity to manage your emotional states.

And it’s almost entirely learned through early relationships.

A securely attached child , one whose emotions were consistently met with calm, attuned responses , develops a limbic system that can self-soothe.

An insecurely attached child , one whose emotions were dismissed, punished, or ignored , develops a limbic system that panics easily and struggles to calm down.

The data is striking: A 30-year longitudinal study from the University of Minnesota found that children with secure early attachments had: - 63% less anxiety in adulthood - 58% better emotional regulation - 47% healthier romantic relationships Not because they had perfect lives. But because their limbic systems learned early: Emotions are safe. I can feel them and survive them.

For those who didn’t get that programming?

The parent brain stays in overdrive- Constantly vigilant. Never quite trusting that everything’s okay.

THE NEOCORTEX: THE BOSS

And on top of both the reptilian and limbic brain , only 200 thousand years old , sits the neocortex, your thinking brain.

It plans, reasons, imagines. It’s the boss in the room , calm, strategic, future-focused.

The neocortex is what separates us from other mammals. It's why we can write poetry, build rockets, contemplate our own existence.

It's why we can choose not to react to every impulse.

The Prefrontal Cortex , the VIP section of the neocortex , is particularly important.

This is your executive function center.

Decision-making, impulse control, emotional regulation, planning, problem-solving.

Everything that makes you feel like a functional adult.

When neuroscientists scan the brains of people making difficult decisions, they see the prefrontal cortex light up like a Christmas tree. It's weighing options, considering consequences, overriding immediate impulses.

Dr. Daniel Siegel, clinical professor of psychiatry at UCLA, describes the prefrontal cortex as having nine key functions: 1. Body regulation 2. Attuned communication 3. Emotional balance 4. Response flexibility (not just reacting)

5. Fear modulation (calming the amygdala)

6. Empathy 7. Insight (self-awareness)

8. Moral awareness 9. Intuition When this part is online...

When the boss is present...

You lead your life instead of reacting to the threats around you.

But Here's the Problem

The prefrontal cortex is the slowest part of your brain. It's thoughtful, deliberate, energy- intensive. It takes time to analyze a situation and formulate a response.

The reptilian brain and limbic system?

They're fast. Lightning fast.

They evolved to be fast because hesitation meant death.

So, when you're stressed, scared, or overwhelmed , The fast brain takes over.

The slow brain gets drowned out.

A landmark 2015 study from the Salk Institute found that under high stress, the prefrontal cortex essentially goes offline.

Blood flow and neural activity shift to the amygdala and brainstem. The boss gets kicked out of the meeting.

That's why you say things you regret when you're angry. Why you make terrible decisions when you're anxious. Why you can't think clearly when you're panicking.

The child and the parent are running the show. And they're not good at strategy.

THE FAMILY DYNAMICS

Together these three parts of the brain form a family: • Reptilian brain , the child: impulsive, reactive, always scanning for threat • Limbic system , the parent: emotional, protective, easily overwhelmed • Neocortex , the boss: steady, intelligent, capable of seeing the bigger picture When life shakes you, the child panics , Tiger! Run! Hide! Danger!

The parent over-protects

You can't trust anyone. Everyone leaves. You're not safe. „ And the boss , your prefrontal cortex , gets drowned out.

That's anxiety.

Not weakness , just wiring.

The primitive brain shouts louder because it's older and faster. More aggressive. Trained to kill the tiger in the jungle or cower in fear from being eaten.

A Day in the Life of Your Brain Let me show you how this plays out.

Scenario: You send a vulnerable text to someone you care about …

Hours pass…

No response…

The Child (Reptilian Brain) reacts first: Danger! Rejection! They hate me! I'm being abandoned!

Heart rate spikes.

Breathing shallows.

Stomach clenches.

The Parent (Limbic System) joins in: I knew this would happen. It always happens.

Everyone leaves. I'm unlovable.

Memories flood in , every past rejection, every time you felt unwanted.

Emotions surge , shame, fear, grief.

The Boss (Neocortex) tries to intervene: Wait. Maybe they're just busy. Maybe their phone died. This doesn't mean what the child thinks it means.

But if the child and parent are screaming loud enough , The boss can't get a word in.

You spiral. You catastrophize. You write seventeen draft replies and delete and maybe even block them all.

Until finally, three hours later, they text back: "Sorry, was in a meeting. Miss you."

And suddenly the boss is back online. See? It was nothing. We panicked for no reason.

But the child and parent don't apologize.

They just file this away as another data point: Silence = danger = panic = survival strategy activated.

THE LANGUAGE YOUR BRAIN DOESN'T UNDERSTAND

Your brain also clings to what's familiar. In fact, the human brain is genetically programmed to cling to what is familiar.

Remember the danger from the tigers in the jungle that your ancestors struggled to be safe from- scenario? Even chaos feels safer than change. What if we tried another response instead of fight or flight and were eaten alive instead? It's why we repeat old patterns , they're predictable.

And the brain, bless it, or reprogram it, doesn't understand negatives.

This is crucial, so pay attention.

Say "Don't panic," and your brain hears panic.

Say "Don't fail," and it fixates on fail.

Say "Don't think about a pink elephant"

And guess what you're thinking about?

The Pink Elephant Problem

Neurolinguist George Lakoff conducted

famous experiments showing that the brain can't process negative commands without first activating the concept being negated.

To understand "Don't think of X," your brain must first think of X.

Then try to suppress it.

Which ironically makes you think about it more.

It's like trying to not look at an accident on the highway. The instruction itself draws your attention to it.

A 2014 study from Trinity College Dublin tracked athletes and found that those given negative instructions , "Don't miss," "Don't drop the ball" , performed 34% worse than those given positive ones like "Make the shot,"

"Catch securely"

The brain doesn't process no or not , it just obeys the picture your words paint.

Speak in Pictures, Not Problems So, speak to it in clear, affirmative instructions.

Instead of "I won't mess this up," say "I'm going to get this right."

Instead of "Don't freeze," say "I'm steady."

Instead of "I'm not anxious," say "I'm calm."

That's not optimism , it's neuroscience.

You're feeding new data to the boss , your neocortex, giving it a clear image to work toward.

Dr. Maxwell Maltz, author of Psycho- Cybernetics, discovered this in the 1960s working with patients recovering from plastic surgery. He found that patients who visualized their desired outcome recovered faster than those who focused on avoiding complications.

The brain is a goal-seeking mechanism.

Give it a target.

Not a list of things to avoid.

CALLING THE BOSS BACK

Your task isn't to silence the reptilian brain.

It's to teach it , retrain it.

To train it to the new world protocol.

To make it understand, respect, and follow the instructions of the boss in the room. The neocortex.

Because when the boss stays calm, the rest of the family settles.

The Science of "Feeling to Heal"

Neuroscientist Dr. Jill Bolte Taylor, who famously documented her own stroke in My Stroke of Insight, discovered something profound ,, When an emotion is triggered , The chemical cascade in your body lasts approximately 90 seconds.

Ninety seconds. That's it. Just 90 seconds. A minute and a half.

That's how long it takes for adrenaline and cortisol to flood and then flush out.

After 90 seconds, if you're still upset?

It's because you're re-triggering the response Replaying the story. Feeding the fire.

What you need to do here? Bring the Boss in.

The Neo Cortex. Ditch the emotion. Let's talk practical. Emotion is never practical.

The 90-Second Rule: If you can simply observe the physical sensation of an emotion for 90 seconds without reacting or storytelling , It will naturally dissipate.

But most of us don't do that. We grab onto the emotion and run with it. We narrate it, justify it, build a case around it. And that keeps the child (panic) and parent ("I'll protect your no matter what") in charge, locking the Boss out of the room.

PRACTICE: CALL THE BOSS BACK IN THE ROOM

When fear hijacks you, call the boss back in the room.

Feel the first wave , the quickened pulse, the shallow breath.

"Say softly, "The child's scared. The parent's worried and being over protective.' Boss, can you please tell me what to do?"

That simple naming act switches power to the boss. The neocortex - the reasoning part of your brain.

Step 1: Breathe Like You Mean It Inhale through your nose for 4 Hold for 2 Exhale through your mouth for 6 The long exhale turns on the parasympathetic system , your body's built-in calm switch

Why this works

Dr. Andrew Huberman, neuroscientist at Stanford, explains that the exhale is directly linked to the vagus nerve. When you exhale longer than you inhale, you activate the vagal brake.

Heart rate slows.

Blood pressure drops. Safety returns.

The amygdala gets the message: We're safe now.

A 2019 study in Cell Reports Medicine found that this 4-2-6 breathing pattern (called "physiological sigh") is the fastest way to reduce stress in real-time.

More effective than meditation.

More effective than mindfulness.

More effective than counting to ten.

Step 2: Speak One Believable Line "I'm safe right now."

"I'm handling this."

"I can take one step."

The brain listens to tone and repetition more than drama. Don't shout affirmations.

Don't try to convince yourself of something you don't believe.

Just state a simple, provable truth.

Right now, in this moment, I am physically safe.

Right now, I am breathing.

Right now, I can stand.

That's not spiritual bypassing or gaslighting.

That's anchoring the boss in present-moment reality.

Because the child and parent live in the past and future.

Only the boss lives now.

Step 3: Ground Yourself Move a little, stretch, stand, look around. Its important. Why?

The reptilian brain reads that motion as proof: no tiger here! You are safe to move!

Somatic grounding techniques

Feel your feet on the floor , press down intentionally Touch something with texture , fabric, wood, water.

Name five things you can see, four you can hear, three you can touch, two you can smell, one you can taste (5-4-3-2-1 technique)

Dr. Peter Levine, who developed Somatic Experiencing therapy, found that trauma and anxiety live in the body. Not just the mind.

And that physical movement, especially gentle, intentional movement, helps discharge stuck nervous system activation.

Animals in the wild do this naturally.

After escaping a predator, they shake, tremor, and then return to calm.

Humans have largely lost this instinct.

But we can relearn it

THE 30-SECOND RESET

Thirty seconds.

That's all it takes to bring the boss back online.

Each time you do, you're retraining the child and the parent to trust that calm voice again.

The Mechanism

Neuroscientists call this "top-down regulation." The prefrontal cortex sending inhibitory signals to the amygdala.

Literally telling it to quiet down.

The more you practice this , The stronger that connection becomes. The faster the boss can step in.

A 2020 study from UC Berkeley tracked people practicing daily "emotional regulation exercises" (essentially calling the boss back)

After 30 days: Amygdala reactivity decreased by 31% Prefrontal cortex activation during stress increased by 28% Self-reported anxiety dropped by 42% You're no longer just fighting your biology.

You're leading it.

The child learns safety.

The parent learns balance.

And the boss, the neocortex, now has permission from both the child and the parent.

No longer wary of stepping on anyone's toes or crossing boundaries, it stays steady, patient, result-oriented, and present.

It stays in the room. That's how fear stops running your life.

THE FAMILY COUNCIL

Think of this practice as a daily family meeting.

The child will always be petulant and reactive, that's its job. It's biology.

The parent will always be protective, that's its job, its evolutionary.

But the boss gets to make the final decisions – that's revolutionary.

The boss does not make its decisions independently. Or selfishly. Not by silencing the others.

But by acknowledging them first.

"I hear you, child. You're scared. Thank you for trying to keep me safe."

"I hear you, parent. You're worried. Thank you for caring so much."

"But I've got this. I'm the boss. And I say we're okay."

This isn't suppression. It's integration.

Dr. Dan Siegel calls this "name it to tame it".

When you label what you're feeling , When you acknowledge the different parts of yourself , The prefrontal cortex lights up , And the amygdala calms down.

A 2007 UCLA study using fMRI scans found that simply putting feelings into words , "I'm feeling anxious," or, "The child is panicking"- Reduced amygdala activity by up to 50%.

Language regulates emotion.

YOUR DAILY FAMILY CHECK-IN

Before bed, ask yourself: Who was in charge today?

Did the child run the show?

Reactive, impulsive, driven by fear?

Did the parent dominate?

Overprotective, ruminating, unable to let go?

Telling you exactly what to do, stemming from their own fears and doubts?

Or did the boss lead? Your neocortex.

Calm, clear, making intentional choices?

There's no judgment here.

Just awareness.

Because awareness is how the boss strengthens. Your boss is the neocortex.

Every time you notice who's in charge, and choose not to hand control over to fear or overprotectiveness, the neocortex strengthens. You're giving the boss -your neocortex more power. No more running away from the tigers fear. The neocortex is where your conscious power lives.

In the next chapter, we'll learn exactly how to reprogram the system , how neuroplasticity lets you rewrite the old code and install new software , one breath, one thought, one moment at a time.

PAUSE & PRACTICE: Meet Your Family Sit comfortably.

Close your eyes.

Take three slow breaths.

Now, recall a recent moment of stress.

Notice what happens in your body.

Ask: Where do I feel this? (That's the child speaking through sensation)

What story am I telling myself? (That's the parent speaking through memory)

What do I actually know to be true right now?

(That's the boss speaking through clarity)

Practice recognizing these three voices.

They'll become familiar, and easier to trust.

And when you can identify them?

You can choose which one gets to decide.

The boss is always available.

You just have to invite it back into the room.

CHAPTER 3

REPROGRAMMING THE SYSTEM: THE SCIENCE OF REWIRING YOUR BRAIN.

By now you know the family inside your head.

The child, the parent, and the boss.

Neuroplasticity is how the boss earns lasting authority over the child and the parent. It's the process that lets your brain change its mind about itself and its primordial conditioning.

WHAT IS NEUROPLASTICITY, REALLY?

Neuroplasticity simply means the brain rewires in response to experience , every thought, emotion, or behavior you repeat becomes a road it learns to drive automatically.

Your mind is not fixed. It's a living circuit board, updating constantly.

For most of human history, scientists believed the adult brain was essentially "set" after childhood. Done growing. Done changing.

Hardwired.

If you were anxious at 25, you'd be anxious at 75. If you were depressed in your twenties, good luck in your sixties. They were wrong.

The Breakthrough

In the 1960s and 70s, a handful of rebel neuroscientists started questioning this dogma. Dr. Michael Merzenich at UC San Francisco conducted experiments showing that adult monkey brains could reorganize themselves after injury.

New neural pathways formed.

Functions that were lost could be relearned.

Then came the famous "London taxi driver study".

In 2000, Dr. Eleanor Maguire at University College London scanned the brains of London cab drivers. These drivers spend years memorizing over 25,000 streets in one of the world's most complex cities.

The result? Their hippocampi (the brain's mapping region) were significantly larger than average. Not because they were born with bigger hippocampi. But because they'd grown them through practice.

And here's what is most interesting: The longer they'd been driving, the bigger the hippocampus.

The brain physically changes in response to what you do.

A 2014 study from Harvard took this even further. They taught people to juggle.

After just six weeks, MRI scans showed increased gray matter in areas responsible for visual motion processing. The brain had literally restructured itself to accommodate a new skill.

But when the participants stopped juggling for three months, the gray matter decreased.

Use it or lose it isn't just a saying.

It's neuroscience.

HEBBIAN LEARNING: NEURONS THAT FIRE TOGETHER, WIRE TOGETHER

In 1949, psychologist Donald Hebb proposed what became one of neuroscience's most important principles: "Neurons that fire together, wire together."

When you repeat an experience , a thought, an action, an emotion , the neurons involved in that experience strengthen their connections.

Think of it like this: The first time you think a thought, it's like walking through a field of tall grass. There's no path yet. It takes effort.

The second time, the grass is slightly bent.

Still requires work, but it's easier.

By the tenth time, there's a faint trail.

By the hundredth, a clear path.

By the thousandth, a paved road.

Eventually, the thought becomes automatic.

A highway.

This is why habits are so hard to break.

You've paved a six-lane superhighway.

And your brain loves efficiency.

But here's the beautiful part: If you stop using the highway and start walking a new path.

The old highway gets overgrown. Neural connections that aren't used get "pruned" away.

Neuroscientists call this synaptic pruning.

Your brain's way of saying, "We're not using this anymore. Let's redirect resources elsewhere."

The Timeline of Neural Change

A comprehensive 2018 review in Frontiers in Human Neuroscience mapped the timeline of neuroplastic change: Days 1-3: Initial neural activation: Your brain is trying out the new behavior.

It's effortful, unfamiliar, requires conscious attention.

Days 4-21: Synaptic strengthening begins.

The connections between neurons involved in the new behavior start to solidify.

It's still effortful, but slightly less so.

Days 22-63: Myelination increases.

Myelin is the fatty sheath that wraps around neural connections, making signals travel faster.

This is when the new behavior starts to feel more natural.

Day 64 onwards: Automaticity.

The behavior becomes default.

You don't have to think about it anymore.

The highway is paved.

This is why the old wisdom says "it takes 21 days to form a habit"

Science says it's closer to 66 days on average.

But the range is anywhere from 18 to 254 days, depending on the complexity of the behavior and the individual.

The point

Change is possible.

But it requires consistency over time.

THE THREE INGREDIENTS OF REWIRING

When you introduce new, steady thoughts and pair them with safety , calm breath, small action, genuine relief , the adult brain sends new electrical patterns through the system.

Those signals travel downward, calming the emotional parent and the primitive child.

Over time, the lower layers learn: we can relax now; we're safe again.

That's why healing takes practice. You're not convincing yourself with words , you're showing your neurons new routes to travel until they forget the old ones.

Three ingredients shape every new neural pathway:

1. REPETITION

The brain learns by frequency, not drama.

A small, calm thought repeated daily matters more than a grand revelation felt once.

The Science

Dr. Lara Boyd, neuroscientist at the University of British Columbia, conducted a fascinating study on motor learning.

She found that people who practiced a new skill for 10 minutes every day showed more neural change than those who practiced for 70 minutes once a week.

Even though the total practice time was the same.

Why?

Because the brain consolidates learning during rest. Especially during sleep.

When you practice something, then sleep, then practice again? You're giving the brain multiple opportunities to strengthen the connection.

One intense session doesn't do that. It's like trying to water a plant by dumping a bucket on it once a month , versus giving it a little water every day.

Consistency beats intensity.

2. EMOTION

The limbic system decides what's worth remembering. When a new behavior feels good, meaningful, or peaceful , the signal deepens.

The Science of Emotional Tagging

Dr. James McGaugh at UC Irvine discovered that emotional experiences trigger the release of norepinephrine in the amygdala.

This acts like a "save this" button in your brain. Neutral experiences might get filed away, but emotional ones get marked as important.

That's why you remember your wedding day in vivid detail. But not what you ate for breakfast six days ago.

Application: When you're trying to rewire your brain, you need to make the new behavior feel good. Not forced. Not like punishment. But genuinely pleasant.

That's why breathwork paired with gratitude is more powerful than breathwork alone.

That's why movement with music rewires faster than movement in silence.

That's why affirmations with a hand on your heart feel different than affirmations muttered mechanically.

You're giving the limbic system a reason to care.

3. SAFETY

The primitive brain only learns when it's calm. That's why you can't grow under threat , your neurons are too busy defending themselves.

The Neuroscience of Safety

Dr. Stephen Porges' Polyvagal Theory explains this beautifully When your nervous system is in threat mode (sympathetic activation or dorsal vagal shutdown), the brain prioritizes survival over learning. Neuroplasticity essentially shuts down. Because why would you waste energy learning when you might just die the next minute?

But when your nervous system is in safety mode (ventral vagal activation) the prefrontal cortex comes online. The hippocampus can encode new memories.

Neural growth factors like BDNF (Brain- Derived Neurotrophic Factor) get released.

Neuroplasticity is activated.

Brain-Derived Neurotrophic Factor

(BDNF) is like miracle-gro for your neurons It promotes the growth of new neurons and strengthens existing connections.

A 2016 study in Nature Reviews Neuroscience found that stress reduces BDNF.

While activities like exercise, meditation, and social connection increase it.

Translation: You cannot hate yourself into growth.

You cannot shame yourself into healing.

You cannot terrify yourself into change.

The nervous system doesn't work that way.

Pair these together , repetition, emotion, and safety , and you've created the perfect chemical conditions for change. That is the essence of Calm Sutra.

THE TWO-MINUTE REWIRE

This is how you translate theory into biology Step 1: Find a Quiet Minute Sit, stand, or walk , it doesn't matter.

Let your shoulders drop.

Release your jaw.

Soften your belly.

You're signaling to the nervous system: It's safe to be here.

Step 2: Anchor with Breath Inhale gently for four counts.

Hold for two.

Exhale for six.

Feel the pulse slow.

That's your vagus nerve flipping the brain from alarm to learning mode.

Why this breath pattern specifically: Dr. Andrew Huberman explains that the physiological sigh (double inhale followed by long exhale) is hardwired into our nervous system.

Even newborn babies do it. It's the fastest biological way to offload CO2 and reduce anxiety.

But for rewiring purposes, the 4-2-6 pattern works beautifully because: The inhale activates the sympathetic system (just slightly)

The hold creates a pause (allowing you to observe)

The long exhale activates the parasympathetic system (creating safety)

It's a mini-arc of activation and regulation.

A complete cycle.

Step 3: Feed One New Line to the System Choose a phrase you want the adult brain to teach the rest: "I can handle this."

"I'm safe right now."

"I'm learning how to stay calm."

Say it slowly, with feeling , The limbic brain needs tone, not perfection.

The Language of Rewiring

Notice these phrases are: 1. Present-tense , not "I will be" but "I am"

2. Believable , not "I'm perfectly calm"

(which you know is a lie) but "I'm learning to be calm" (which is true)

3. Affirmative , not "I'm not anxious" but "I'm steady"

You're not trying to gaslight your nervous system. You're giving it a new story that it can actually believe.

Step 4: Add a Micro-Action Straighten your back.

Lift your chin.

Open your chest.

Place a hand on your heart.

A physical cue that tells the primitive brain, no threat detected.

Embodied Cognition

A 2012 study from Ohio State University found that body posture directly influences thought patterns.

People who sat up straight while writing about themselves used more confident, positive language than those who were slouched.

This isn't "fake it till you make it"

This is body-to-brain signaling.

Your posture literally sends messages to your nervous system.

Collapsed chest = vulnerability, threat, need protection.

Open chest = confidence, safety, I've got this.

Amy Cuddy's famous "power pose" research may have been criticized for overstating effects. But the core finding holds up: How you hold your body influences how you feel.

THE REPETITION RULE

That's it.

Two minutes, once or twice a day.

Each repetition strengthens the new connection between thought, breath, and body.

You're pairing a mental message with a physical signal of safety , the exact formula that rewires the fear circuits.

Why "once or twice a day" specifically: Because the brain consolidates learning during rest and sleep.

If you do this practice once in the morning , your brain processes it during the day and especially during your next sleep cycle.

If you do it again in the evening , You're giving the brain two consolidation opportunities in 24 hours.

After 30 days of this, brain scans show:

Decreased amygdala reactivity

Increased prefrontal cortex thickness Improved vagal tone (the efficiency of your calm-down system)

This isn't spiritual.

This is structural change.

THE LONG GAME: WHAT HAPPENS OVER TIME

Let me show you what consistent practice actually looks like in the brain.

Weeks 1-2: The Awareness Phase You're mostly just remembering to do the practice. It feels awkward. The child and parent are skeptical. "This is stupid. This won't work. What's the point?"

What's happening in the brain: Initial neural activation.

You're creating the faint path in the tall grass.

The connections are weak, easily disrupted.

Don't be discouraged , this is the hardest phase , because nothing feels different yet.

Weeks 3-4: The Noticing Phase You start to notice tiny shifts.

Maybe you don't spiral as deeply into anxiety.

Maybe you catch yourself catastrophizing and pause.

Maybe one day, you just feel a little lighter.

What's happening

Synaptic strengthening. The neurons that fire during your practice are starting to wire together. The path is becoming visible.

Weeks 5-8: The Integration Phase The practice starts to feel more natural.

Less like "doing" something and more like "being" something. You might even start doing it automatically when stressed without having to remember.

What's happening

Myelination.

The connections are getting insulated, making the signal travel faster.

The new highway is being paved.

Months 3-6: The Identity Shift This is when people say, "I don't know what changed, but something's different"

You don't identify as "an anxious person trying to be calm" anymore.

You just... feel steadier...

More yourself.

What's happening

The new neural pathway has become default.

The old anxiety highway is getting overgrown from disuse.

Your brain has literally restructured itself.

A 2019 longitudinal study from UCLA tracked people practicing daily mindfulness for six months.

Brain scans showed: - 30% reduction in amygdala volume (less reactive fear center), 15% increase in prefrontal cortex thickness (stronger boss), significantly improved vagal tone, and changes in gene expression related to inflammation and immune response They weren't just thinking differently.

They were now biologically different too.

THE RESISTANCE: WHY YOUR BRAIN FIGHTS CHANGE

Here's the thing nobody tells you.

Your brain will resist this.

Not because it's broken.

But because it's protecting you.

The Predictive Brain

Your brain is a prediction machine.

It's constantly trying to anticipate what will happen next , based on what happened before.

Dr. Lisa Feldman Barrett, neuroscientist at Northeastern University, calls this the "predictive processing" model. Your brain creates a simulation of reality based on past experience. Then checks incoming sensory data against that simulation.

When reality matches prediction = no alarm When reality doesn't match prediction = alert!

pay attention! something's different!

This is why change feels uncomfortable.

Even good change.

Your brain interprets "different" as "potentially dangerous" Because in our evolutionary past, "different" often was.

The Comfort of Discomfort

This is why people stay in toxic relationships.

Why they self-sabotage success. Why they return to old patterns even after swearing they won't.

It's not weakness.

It's prediction error minimization.

Your brain would rather be right about its predictions , even if those predictions are painful , than be surprised.

A 2017 study from MIT found that the brain experiences more stress when positive unexpected things happen than when negative expected things happen.

Read that again.

Unexpected good news is more stressful than expected bad news!

Because the brain can prepare for expected bad news , but it doesn't know what to do with unexpected good news.

That's why lottery winners often report feeling anxious.

Why promotions can trigger impostor syndrome.

Why falling in love can feel terrifying.

Your nervous system is screaming, "This doesn't match my predictions! Danger!"

HOW THE BOSS TAKES THE WHEEL

This is how the adult takes the wheel again: by showing up, quietly, repeatedly, until the child and the parent trust it enough to rest.

You don't need to shout affirmations.

You don't need to erase old memories.

You just need to keep sending calm signals through the system , until calm becomes familiar.

That's the real work of unbreaking your mind.

The Trust Timeline

Week 1: The child and parent don't trust the boss at all "You were not there last time. Why should we listen to you now?"

Week 4: "Okay, you've shown up consistently.

But we're still watching."

Week 8: "Maybe you're serious about this."

Week 12: "Okay. We'll let you lead. But if things go wrong, we're taking over again."

Month 6: "You've got this. We'll be here if you need us, but you're in charge now."

This is how custody is earned.

Not through force.

But through consistent, safe presence.

THE PRACTICE TRACKER

To help you stay consistent, I recommend tracking your practice.

Not obsessively , Not as another thing to judge yourself for , But as a simple visual reminder that you're showing up.

Get a calendar or notebook.

Every day you do the Two-Minute Rewire, mark an X.

Aim for at least 5 days a week.

Perfection is not the goal. Consistency is.

Research shows that visible progress tracking increases adherence by 37% Because it gives the brain evidence that change is happening , even when you can't feel it yet.

THE REWIRING PROMISE

Here's what I can promise you: After 30 days of consistent practice: You won't be "cured". But you'll have moments where you notice yourself responding differently.

After 90 days: The new response will start to feel more natural than the old one.

After 6 months: You'll look back and barely recognize the person you were. Not because you've become someone new.

But because you've become more you.

The version of you the fear was covering up.

This isn't magic. It's neuroscience.

And it works. If you work on it.

In the next chapter, we'll explore your inner pharmacy ,, how every emotion you feel is a chemical, how feelings affect your body's health, and how to consciously prescribe yourself the medicine of calm.

PAUSE & PRACTICE: Your First 30-Day Commitment Right now, before you move on, make a contract with yourself.

I commit to practicing the Two-Minute Rewire: Morning, evening, or both.

At least 5 days a week.

For the next 30 days.

Write it down.

Say it out loud.

Tell someone about i.t Because commitment creates accountability.

And accountability strengthens neural pathways.

Your brain is listening.

Give it a clear instruction.

Then show up and follow through.

The boss is ready. Are you?

CHAPTER 4 ,

YOUR INNER PHARMACY:

HOW FEELINGS BECOME CHEMISTRY

AND CHEMISTRY BECOMES HEALTH

Every emotion you feel is a chemical.

Every thought, a prescription you write for your own body.

Your inner world doesn't just stay in your head , it floods your bloodstream.

Joy, fear, resentment, gratitude, each has its own molecular perfume.

This is your inner pharmacy, dispensing doses 24 hours a day. Learn to use it well.

THE CHEMISTRY SET IN YOUR SKULL

Most people think of emotions as abstract, ephemeral things, feelings that happen "in your mind", separate from your body...

Wrong!

Every single emotion is a chemical event.

When you worry, your body mixes a cocktail of cortisol and adrenaline.

When you relax, it releases serotonin and oxytocin.

When you chase goals, dopamine fuels the pursuit.

Every mood is a micro-dose that shapes the health of your heart, immune system, digestion, and sleep.

Dr. Candace Pert, a neuroscientist who discovered the opiate receptor in the brain, spent her career proving that emotions are chemical messengers.

In her groundbreaking book Molecules of Emotion, she wrote: "Your body is your subconscious mind. Our physical body can be changed by the emotions we experience."

Translation: What you feel doesn't just happen in your head.

It happens in your cells.

Your tissues.

Your organs.

Everywhere.

THE MAIN PLAYERS: MEET YOUR NEUROCHEMICALS

CORTISOL: The Alarm Chemical

What it does

Cortisol is your body's main stress hormone.

Designed for short bursts of survival.

When you're in danger, cortisol: Increases blood sugar (for quick energy)

Sharpens focus

Suppresses non-essential functions

(digestion, reproduction, immune response)

Keeps you alert and ready to act When it goes wrong: Chronic release keeps you alert but inflamed.

The damage

Blood sugar rises → risk of diabetes Immunity falls → more infections, slower healing Skin dulls → premature aging Memory problems → hippocampus shrinkage Weight gain (especially around the middle)

Bone density loss

High blood pressure

A 2018 study from the University of California found that people with chronically elevated cortisol had: 37% higher risk of cardiovascular disease 28% higher risk of type 2 diabetes 47% higher risk of depression Fun fact that's not fun at all: Chronic stress can shrink your hippocampus by up to 20%. That's the brain region responsible for memory and emotional regulation. So, stress makes you forgetful and less able to handle... stress!

It's a vicious cycle.

ADRENALINE: The Sprint Hormone

What it does

Adrenaline (also called epinephrine) is cortisol's aggressive cousin.

It:

Increases heart rate

Dilates pupils

Opens airways

Diverts blood to muscles Triggers the release of glucose It's the "fight or flight" chemical. Designed to help you outrun predators or punch your way out of danger.

When it goes wrong: Too much turns into restlessness and anxiety.

Your body is revving the engine but going nowhere...

Chronic adrenaline leads to:

Heart palpitations

Anxiety and panic attacks Insomnia

Digestive issues

Headaches Burnout

The modern problem

Your body releases adrenaline when you check your email. When you scroll bad news.

When you're stuck in traffic. When you argue with your partner.

But you can't run from an email. You can't punch the traffic. So, all that mobilized energy stays trapped in your system. Eating away at your health.

DOPAMINE: The Motivator

What it does

Dopamine is the "I want that" chemical. It lights up when you anticipate reward.

Not when you get the reward. But when you're chasing it.

It's the chemical that makes you:

Set goals

Take action

Feel motivated

Experience pleasure

Learn new things

Balanced dopamine brings

Creativity Focus Drive

Joy in achievement

When it goes wrong: Excess turns into addiction and burnout.

Because dopamine doesn't care what you're chasing , Only that you ARE chasing.

Cocaine, Instagram likes, gambling, work, shopping, sugar, they all hijack the dopamine system.

A Stanford study found that: Social media notifications spike dopamine by 400% Sex spikes it by 200% Food spikes it by 150% Cocaine spikes it by 1000%

The dopamine trap

The more you chase, the more you need to feel the same high. It's called tolerance And it's why nothing feels as good as it used to.

Modern life is essentially a dopamine casino.

Infinite scroll, autoplay, one-click shopping, notifications. All designed to keep you chasing the next hit.

SEROTONIN: The Stabilizer

What it does

Serotonin is the calm, steady, "everything's okay" chemical.

It:

Smooths mood swings

Regulates appetite

Supports healthy sleep

Promotes feelings of contentment Helps with impulse control Healthy serotonin levels correlate with:

Emotional stability

Confidence

Mental clarity

Restful sleep

Healthy digestion (90% of serotonin is made in your gut!)

When it's low

Depression Anxiety Insomnia Irritability Food cravings (especially carbs and sugar)

Obsessive thoughts

What raises serotonin

Sunlight (seriously , 20 minutes of natural light can increase serotonin by 25%)

Gratitude practices

Small social wins (a smile from a stranger, a text from a friend)

Tryptophan-rich foods (turkey, eggs, salmon, nuts, seeds)

Exercise A 2019 study from JAMA Psychiatry found that people who spent at least 2 hours a week in nature had 30% higher serotonin levels than those who didn't.

Nature isn't just pretty. It's medicine.

OXYTOCIN: The Trust Chemical

What it does

Oxytocin is the "love and connection"

hormone.

It's released during

Hugging

Physical touch

Eye contact

Petting animals

Childbirth and breastfeeding

Orgasm

Acts of kindness

What it does to your body:

Lowers blood pressure

Reduces cortisol

Quiets the amygdala (fear center)

Increases trust and empathy

Promotes bonding

Reduces inflammation

Dr. Paul Zak, a neuroeconomist who studies oxytocin, found that even 8 hugs a day can significantly boost oxytocin and improve overall wellbeing.

The modern crisis

We're more "connected" than ever through screens , but more disconnected physically.

Human beings need touch.

A 2020 study during the pandemic found that prolonged social isolation led to: 43% drop in oxytocin levels Corresponding rise in anxiety and depression

Increased inflammation markers

Your body knows the difference between a text message and a hug.

ENDORPHINS: The Body's Natural Painkillers

What they do

Endorphins are your body's morphine.

They dull pain and create euphoria.

What releases them

Movement (the "runner's high")

Music Laughter

Spicy food

Acupuncture Massage Sex A 2017 study from Oxford found that just 15 minutes of laughing releases enough endorphins to raise your pain threshold by 10% That's not metaphorical. Laughter literally makes you more resilient to pain.

WHEN EMOTION BECOMES BIOLOGY

These aren't abstract molecules.

They are the subtle architecture of your vitality , shifting constantly in response to what you feel, think, and do.

Chronic emotion becomes chronic chemistry.

If fear is constant, cortisol stays high and the immune system slows down.

If frustration is daily, blood pressure creeps upward.

If hopelessness lingers, dopamine output falters , the world dulls.

But the reverse is also true.

If you feed the body calm, the body starts believing it.

Lower stress hormones mean less inflammation, steadier energy, clearer thinking.

That's not philosophy , it's biochemistry.

THE IMMUNE SYSTEM CONNECTION

Let me show you how directly emotions impact your immune system.

The PNI Discovery

In the 1970s, psychologist Robert Ader was studying rats. He paired a sweet drink with an immune-suppressing drug. Eventually, the sweet drink alone suppressed the rats'

immune systems , even without the drug.

This launched the field of Psychoneuroimmunology (PNI)

The study of how the mind (psycho), brain (neuro), and immune system (immunology)

talk to each other.

The finding

Your immune system has receptors for neurotransmitters. It's literally listening to your brain.

When you're stressed, your immune cells get the message. And they either go into overdrive (inflammation) or shut down (immunosuppression)

A landmark 1991 study published in the New England Journal of Medicine found that people under high stress were: 5.5 times more likely to develop a cold when exposed to a virus Healed from wounds 40% slower Showed 50% weaker antibody response to vaccines Your emotions are literally programming your immune response.

The Inflammation Connection

Chronic stress creates chronic inflammation And inflammation is the root of almost every modern disease: • Heart disease • Diabetes • Cancer • Alzheimer's • Autoimmune conditions • Depression (yes, depression is now considered an inflammatory condition)

A 2019 study from Carnegie Mellon found that people with high stress had 53% higher levels of inflammatory markers (like IL-6 and CRP) in their blood.

Translation: Chronic worry is setting your body on fire Slowly Silently At the cellular level

The Gene Expression Factor

Dr. Bruce Lipton, cellular biologist, discovered that stress can change which genes get expressed.

You can't change your DNA. But you can change which genes get turned on or off.

This is called epigenetics.

A 2013 study from UCLA found that people who practiced meditation for 8 weeks showed measurable changes in gene expression Specifically: Genes related to inflammation were downregulated (turned off)

Genes related to immune response were upregulated (turned on)

They didn't meditate their DNA They meditated their gene expression Emotions don't just affect how you feel They affect how your cells behave

THE FIVE-MINUTE CHEMICAL TUNE-UP

Here's how to consciously shift your inner pharmacy.

From stress chemicals to calm chemicals.

In five minutes.

Step 1: MOVE Shake out your hands

Roll your shoulders

Stretch open the chest Movement releases endorphins and signals safety to the nervous system.

Why moving works

When you're stressed, your muscles tense in preparation for fight or flight.

But if you never actually fight or flee, that tension stays stuck.

Shaking and stretching tells your body: "The threat is over. We can discharge this now."

Animals do this instinctively after escaping predators. They shake, tremor, then go back to grazing. Humans need to remember to do it.

A 2018 study found that just two minutes of shaking and stretching reduced cortisol by 11% Step 2: BREATHE Inhale through the nose for 4 seconds Hold for 2 Exhale slowly through the mouth for 6 This ratio drops cortisol and activates the vagus nerve , your inner brake pedal.

The mechanism

Long exhales stimulate the parasympathetic nervous system

Heart rate slows

Blood pressure drops

Digestive function resumes

Immune function improves

Five minutes. That's all it takes.

That's faster than making coffee.

Step 3: FEEL SOMETHING GOOD ON PURPOSE Recall one moment , recent or distant that made you feel ease.

Let that memory live for a few breaths.

Serotonin and oxytocin begin to rise

Why this works

Your brain doesn't know the difference between a memory and reality.

When you vividly recall a pleasant memory, the same neurochemicals that were present then get released now.

Dr. Rick Hanson, neuropsychologist, calls this "taking in the good" And he found that spending just 20 seconds dwelling on a positive memory is enough to begin rewiring your brain toward positivity.

The instructions

Close your eyes

Recall a specific moment when you felt safe, loved, or joyful Don't just think about it

Feel it

Where in your body did that feeling live?

Chest? Belly? Throat?

Breathe into that space Step 4: SMILE , Even Slightly The facial muscles loop back to the brain They tell it, "We're okay."

Dopamine answers

The facial feedback hypothesis: Developed by psychologist Paul Ekman, this theory states that the act of smiling causes positive feelings. Not just reflects them.

In a now-famous 2012 study, participants were asked to hold chopsticks in their mouths in a way that forced their faces into a smile.

They didn't know they were smiling, but their stress levels dropped and their mood improved.

Your face is a remote control for your brain.

Even a fake smile can trick your system into releasing feel-good chemicals.

But a genuine smile , one that reaches your eyes (called a Duchenne smile) , is even more powerful.

Step 5: REPEAT DAILY Five minutes of chemical awareness can rebalance hours of emotional noise.

Why daily

Because neurotransmitter levels fluctuate throughout the day You're not creating permanent change with one session You're training your system to default to calm

Consistency over intensity

THE MIND-BODY LOOP

What you think, you feel What you feel, you secrete What you secrete, you become The beauty of the body is that it's listening...

constantly.

It believes the tone of your inner voice, not its logic. That's why soft thoughts heal faster than harsh ones.

The Self-Talk Study

Dr. Ethan Kross at the University of Michigan conducted a fascinating study on self-talk.

He found that people who spoke to themselves in the third person ("Ethan can handle this") or second person ("You've got this") during stressful situations showed:

Lower cortisol

Better performance

Less emotional reactivity

Why?

Because third-person self-talk creates psychological distance „ It activates the prefrontal cortex (the boss)

instead of the amygdala (the child) „ First person: "I'm freaking out!" = emotional, reactive, amygdala-driven Third person: "She's feeling anxious right now" = observational, calm, prefrontal-driven

Try it

Instead of "I can't do this" „ Say "[Your name] is learning how to do this"

Notice the shift

EMOTIONAL HYGIENE IS PHYSICAL HYGIENE

Most people brush their teeth twice a day

Take a shower

Wash their hands

But how many practice emotional hygiene?

If you don't process your emotions If you don't release stress If you don't flush cortisol and rebalance your system It's like never brushing your teeth Eventually, things rot Peace is preventive medicine.

A comprehensive 2016 review in Psychosomatic Medicine analyzed 200+ studies on mind-body interventions and found: People who practiced daily emotional regulation (meditation, breathwork, journaling) had: 32% lower all-cause mortality 43% lower risk of heart disease 29% better immune function 47% less chronic pain 51% lower rates of depression and anxiety

That's not placebo

That's measurable, biological change

THE CHEMICAL CASCADES

Let me show you how one emotion cascades through your entire system.

The Stress Cascade

Thought: I'm going to fail this presentation 0.2 seconds later: Amygdala activates → signals hypothalamus → releases CRH (corticotropin-releasing hormone)

5 seconds later:

Pituitary gland releases ACTH

(adrenocorticotropic hormone)

30 seconds later: Adrenal glands release cortisol and adrenaline

Physical response

Heart rate increases (from 70 to 110 bpm)

Blood pressure spikes

Digestion shuts down

Muscles tense

Pupils dilate

Palms sweat

Mind races

If repeated daily for months:

Hippocampus shrinks

Prefrontal cortex thins

Amygdala enlarges

Chronic inflammation

Weakened immune system

Disrupted sleep

Accelerated aging

All from a thought!

The Calm Cascade

Thought: I am safe right now Immediate: Prefrontal cortex activates → sends inhibitory signals to amygdala

Within seconds

Vagus nerve stimulated → parasympathetic activation

Within minutes

Heart rate decreases

Blood pressure normalizes

Digestion resumes

Muscles relax

Breathing deepens

Oxytocin and serotonin release If repeated daily for months: Increased vagal tone (better stress resilience)

Thicker prefrontal cortex

Smaller, less reactive amygdala

Lower baseline cortisol

Stronger immune function

Better sleep

Slower aging

Same system

Different input

Radically different outcome

YOU DON'T HAVE TO SILENCE EMOTION

Let me be clear. This isn't about suppressing or denying what you feel.

Emotional suppression is toxic.

A 2013 Stanford study found that people who chronically suppressed emotions had:

Higher cortisol

Worse memory

More relationship problems

Increased risk of early death You're not trying to eliminate emotions You're trying to metabolize them Think of emotions like food.

You need to digest them. Not ignore them until they rot.

The practice

Feel it

Name it

Let it move through Then consciously shift your chemistry

THE PRESCRIPTION YOU WRITE YOURSELF

Every day, you're prescribing Worry = cortisol and adrenaline Gratitude = serotonin and oxytocin Connection = oxytocin Movement = endorphins and dopamine Stress = cortisol Laughter = endorphins Nature = serotonin Calm breathing = parasympathetic activation You are both the pharmacist and the patient.

The question isn't whether you'll dispense chemicals.

You will. Your body does it automatically based on your emotions.

The question is: Which chemicals are you choosing?

In the next chapter, we'll move from internal chemistry to integration , how to live with this awareness in motion: work, relationships, stress, and the endless hum of the world.

Because calm isn't isolation; it's chemistry practiced in chaos.

PAUSE & PRACTICE: Your Daily Chemical Cocktail For the next seven days, track your emotional chemistry Morning: What emotional state did you wake up in?

What chemicals were you brewing?

(Anxious = cortisol, Excited = dopamine, Peaceful = serotonin, etc.)

Midday check-in

What shifted?

What triggered it?

Evening reflection

What was your dominant emotional chemistry today?

Did you consciously shift it at any point?

Or did you just ride the wave?

Awareness is the first step to authorship You can't change what you don't notice.

So, start noticing.

CHAPTER 5 , THE VAGUS NERVE: YOUR BODY'S SECRET RESET BUTTON

Here's something that nobody taught you in school.

Running through your body is a superhighway of calm.

A nerve that connects your brain to almost every major organ. And it has the power to override your entire stress response.

Meet the vagus nerve.

Your body's built-in chill pill.

WHAT IS THE VAGUS NERVE?

The vagus nerve is the longest cranial nerve in your body. It starts at the base of your skull and wanders (that's what "vagus" means , wanderer) down through your neck, chest, and abdomen.

It touches

Your heart

Your lungs

Your digestive system

Your liver

Your spleen

Your kidneys

It's the main highway of your parasympathetic nervous system , the rest-and-digest mode.

While the sympathetic nervous system is your gas pedal (fight-or-flight), the vagus nerve is your brake pedal.

THE TWO-WAY STREET

Here's what's fascinating. The vagus nerve is 90% afferent.

Afferent means carrying toward a center (like sensory info to the brain or blood to an organ), while efferent means carrying away from a center (like motor commands from the brain or blood away from an organ).

So yes, the vagus nerve is 90% afferent.

Which means: 90% of the signals travel FROM your body TO your brain.

Only 10% go the other way i.e. from your brain to your body.

Read that again.

Your body has nine times more influence over your brain than your brain has over your body!

Your gut literally talks to your brain more than your brain talks to your gut.

This is why

You get butterflies in your stomach when nervous Your chest tightens when sad Your throat closes when you're about to cry You feel a "gut feeling" about decisions

That's not metaphor

That's the vagus nerve transmitting data Dr. Stephen Porges, who developed Polyvagal Theory, discovered that the vagus nerve is constantly scanning your internal state and sending reports to your brain.

"Am I safe?"

"Is my heart beating too fast?"

"Is digestion happening?"

"Are we breathing okay?"

Your brain then interprets these signals and decides: Are we safe? Or are we in danger?

This unconscious scanning is called neuroception. And it determines whether you feel calm or anxious.

Often before you're consciously aware of why.

THE THREE BRANCHES OF THE VAGUS

Porges discovered that the vagus nerve isn't just one thing. It has three branches that evolved at different times in our history.

The Dorsal Vagal: The Shutdown Response Age: ~500 million years old (reptilian)

This is the most primitive branch

It governs immobilization

When threat is overwhelming and you can't fight or flee -this kicks in.

Physical effects

Dissociation Numbness Collapse Fainting

Digestive shutdown

Feeling disconnected from your body

When it activates

Extreme trauma

Overwhelming helplessness

Prolonged, inescapable stress Think of it as the emergency shutdown. When nothing else works, the system goes offline.

This is why trauma survivors sometimes report feeling "frozen" or "not there" during the traumatic event.

It's not a choice. It's ancient biology.

The Sympathetic: The Mobilization Response Age: ~200 million years old (early mammals)

This is your fight-or-flight system We talked about it in Chapter 1

Physical effects

Increased heart rate

Rapid breathing

Sweating

Muscle tension

Heightened alertness

Adrenaline and cortisol release

When it activates

Perceived threat

Deadlines Conflict Fear Excitement It's not bad. It's adaptive for short-term challenges. But chronic activation is what kills us.

The Ventral Vagal: The Social Engagement System Age: ~200,000 years old (modern humans)

This is the newest branch And the most uniquely human

Physical effects

Calm, regulated heart rate Deep, easy breathing

Relaxed muscles

Good digestion

Open, expressive face Warm, attuned connection with others Ability to learn, play, and create

When it's active

You feel safe

You can be present You can connect with others You can think clearly You can be creative

You can heal

This is your optimal state

Where neuroplasticity happens

Where healing happens

Where growth happens

VAGAL TONE: YOUR CALM CAPACITY

Just like you can strengthen muscles, you can strengthen your vagus nerve.

This is called vagal tone. And it's a measure of how quickly you can shift from stress to calm.

High vagal tone means: You recover quickly from stress Your heart rate variability (HRV) is high You can regulate emotions effectively

You're resilient

You're socially connected

You're healthier overall

Low vagal tone means: You stay stressed longer You struggle to calm down Emotional regulation is hard You're more prone to anxiety and depression You get sick more often You have more inflammation Studies have found that people with high vagal tone had: 40% lower risk of heart disease 32% lower rates of depression 28% better immune function 53% higher reported life satisfaction Your vagal tone is trainable. Like a bicep for calm.

HOW TO ACTIVATE YOUR VAGUS NERVE

The good news: You can consciously stimulate your vagus nerve.

And flip yourself from fight-or-flight to rest- and-digest in minutes.

1. THE PHYSIOLOGICAL SIGH

We've mentioned this before, but it's worth repeating.

Double inhale through the nose, long exhale through the mouth:

Inhale deeply

Inhale again (a little sip of air)

Long, slow exhale

Why this works

When you inhale, your heart rate speeds up slightly When you exhale, it slows down This is called respiratory sinus arrhythmia The double inhale fully inflates the lungs, especially the tiny air sacs (alveoli) that tend to collapse under stress The long exhale activates the vagus nerve directly Dr. Andrew Huberman from Stanford calls this "the fastest way to shift your state in real time" A 2022 study found that one physiological sigh reduced stress markers as effectively as five minutes of meditation.

One breath. That's it.

2. COLD EXPOSURE

Splash cold water on your face. Or immerse your face in cold water for 15-30 seconds.

Why this works

Cold on your face activates the mammalian dive reflex. An ancient response that slows your heart rate and shifts blood flow inward.

Directly stimulating the vagus nerve.

Olympic swimmers and Navy SEALs use this technique before high-pressure events.

A 2014 study from the European Journal of Applied Physiology found that cold water immersion: Increased vagal tone by 27% Reduced cortisol by 19% Improved mood scores by 34% You don't need an ice bath or any of that fancy stuff. A sink or a simple bowl and some cold- water work fine.

3. HUMMING, SINGING, AND CHANTING

The vagus nerve runs right past your vocal cords. When you hum or sing, the vibrations directly stimulate it.

Try this

Hum on your exhale Feel the vibration in your throat and chest That buzz is the vagus nerve activating

Why monks chant

The sustained "Om" or other chanting practices create prolonged vagal stimulation

It's not mystical

It's physiological

A 2016 study found that just 5 minutes of humming or chanting: Increased heart rate variability by 23% Reduced anxiety scores by 31% Increased feelings of social connection So, sing in the shower Chant in the car Hum while you cook You're medicating your nervous system

4. GARGLING

Sounds silly. Works beautifully.

Gargle water vigorously for 30 seconds.

The muscles in the back of your throat activate the vagus nerve.

It's been seen and studied that people who gargled twice daily for 30 days showed:

Improved vagal tone

Better mood

Reduced inflammation markers

Add it to your morning routine Brush teeth → gargle → vagus activation

5. SLOW, DIAPHRAGMATIC BREATHING

Breathe deep into your belly, not your chest.

The technique

Place one hand on your chest, one on your belly Inhale slowly through your nose, letting your belly rise (chest stays still)

Exhale slowly, belly falls 4-6 breaths per minute

Why this works

The diaphragm sits right next to the vagus nerve. When you breathe deeply, the movement of the diaphragm mechanically stimulates it.

Plus, slow breathing increases heart rate variability, which is a direct measure of vagal activation.

Daily slow breathing practice:

Lowers blood pressure

Reduces anxiety

Improves sleep quality

Five minutes. Twice a day. Non-negotiable.

6. LAUGHTER

Real, genuine laughter contracts your diaphragm repeatedly, massaging the vagus nerve.

The data

A 2014 study from Loma Linda University found that watching funny videos for 20 minutes:

Increased vagal tone

Lowered cortisol by 39%

Boosted immune function

Released endorphins

Laughter is free medicine. Use it!

7. MASSAGE

Especially neck, shoulders, and feet. These areas have high vagal innervation.

Self-massage works too

Massage the sides of your neck gently Press and release your shoulders

Rub your feet

8. SOCIAL CONNECTION

The ventral vagal system is also called the social engagement system. It's activated by safe, warm human connection.

Eye contact

A genuine smile

A hug

A conversation where you feel seen All of these stimulate the vagus nerve Long term data suggests that people with strong social connections had:

Higher vagal tone

Lower inflammation

Better cardiovascular health

Longer lifespan

Connection isn't just nice. It's biological necessity.

9. YOGA AND STRETCHING

Certain yoga poses compress or stretch areas where the vagus nerve runs.

Particularly effective

Cat-cow (spinal flexion and extension)

Child's pose (gentle compression on the belly)

Legs up the wall (reverses blood flow)

Sphinx or cobra (opens the chest and throat)

Findings published in Medical Hypotheses

proposed that yoga's benefits come primarily from vagal nerve stimulation. Through breath, posture, and the meditative state it induces.

10. PROBIOTICS AND GUT HEALTH

Remember: 90% of vagal signals come FROM your gut TO your brain.

So gut health = vagal health.

The gut-brain axis

Your gut microbiome produces neurotransmitters, including 90% of your body's serotonin, and 50% of your dopamine.

When your gut is inflamed or dysbiotic (imbalanced bacteria), it sends distress signals up the vagus nerve.

Your brain interprets this as anxiety.

People who took probiotics for 8 weeks showed:

Increased vagal tone

Reduced anxiety and depression

Lower cortisol

Feed your gut well Fermented foods, fiber, prebiotics, probiotics You're feeding the nerve that talks to your brain.

VAGAL TONE WORKOUT: THE 7-DAY PROTOCOL

Want to strengthen your vagus nerve? Here's a one-week intensive.

Day 1: Breath 5 minutes of 4-2-6 breathing, twice today Day 2: Cold Splash cold water on your face 3 times End your shower with 30 seconds of cold water Day 3: Sound Hum for 2 minutes, three times today Sing in the shower Chant "Om" 10 times before bed Day 4: Movement 20 minutes of gentle yoga or stretching Focus on cat-cow and child's pose Day 5: Connection

Have at least one face-to-face conversation Hug someone for 20 seconds (if available and appropriate)

Make eye contact and smile at strangers Day 6: Laughter Watch something funny for 20 minutes

Laugh with friends

Don't force it, but seek it out Day 7: Integration Combine everything: breathe, hum, move, connect, laugh After 7 days:

You should notice

- Faster recovery from stress - Better sleep - More emotional stability - Increased energy - Better digestion This isn't magic. This is anatomy.

HEART RATE VARIABILITY: YOUR VAGAL TONE SCOREBOARD

If you want to measure your progress, track your Heart Rate Variability (HRV)

What is HRV?

It's the variation in time between each heartbeat.

Seems weird, right? Shouldn't your heart beat like a metronome?

No.

A healthy heart has variability. Because it's constantly adjusting to your needs.

High HRV = high vagal tone Your heart can speed up when needed and slow down quickly. You're resilient.

Low HRV = low vagal tone Your heart is less flexible. You're stuck in stress mode.

Low HRV is associated with: Higher risk of heart disease Increased anxiety and depression

Worse immune function

Shorter lifespan

How to measure

Use a wearable device (Apple Watch, Oura Ring, WHOOP, etc.)

Or a chest strap monitor with an HRV app.

Check it first thing in the morning. Track trends over weeks.

As you practice vagal stimulation, watch your HRV improve. It's concrete proof that you're changing your biology.

POLYVAGAL LADDER: WHERE ARE YOU?

Dr. Stephen Porges created the "Polyvagal Ladder" to help people identify their current state.

Top Rung: Ventral Vagal (Social Engagement)

Calm Connected Playful Curious Safe Open Present Middle Rung: Sympathetic (Fight or Flight)

Anxious Agitated Restless Angry Hypervigilant

Racing thoughts

Can't sit still

Bottom Rung: Dorsal Vagal (Shutdown)

Numb Exhausted Hopeless Disconnected Heavy

Can't move

Don't care

Where are you right now?

The practice isn't to live at the top rung all the time. That's unrealistic, life happens.

The practice is to notice which rung you're on. And have tools to climb back up.

From Dorsal to Sympathetic: Movement, cold water, loud music
From Sympathetic to Ventral: Breath, humming, connection

THE VAGUS NERVE AS MEDIATOR

One more crucial thing. The vagus nerve is the mediator between your conscious mind and your automatic body.

You can't consciously control your heart rate.

You can't consciously control your digestion.

You can't consciously control your immune response.

But you can control your vagus nerve.

And your vagus nerve can control all those things.

This is the bridge , Between what you think and what your body does , Between mind and biology.

When you breathe slowly

When you hum

When you connect with others

When you laugh

You're not just "feeling better" You're sending electrical signals down a physical nerve that changes actual biological functions.

Your heart rate literally slows Your digestion literally improves Your immune system literally strengthens This isn't placebo. This is neurobiology.

YOUR RESET BUTTON

The vagus nerve is your biological reset button.

When you're stuck in stress When anxiety is spiraling When your body won't calm down You have a nerve, a physical, measurable nerve that you can activate to flip the switch.

Press the button

Breathe Hum

Splash cold water

Laugh Connect Your body will respond. Not eventually. It will respond immediately.

In the next chapter, we'll explore sleep , the nightly reset that either heals you or harms you , and how the vagus nerve plays a starring role in whether you rest or ruminate.

PAUSE & PRACTICE: Your Daily Vagal Practice Choose three vagal activation techniques from this chapter Morning: Pick one technique and do it for 2-5 minutes Midday: Pick a different one when you feel stress building Evening: Pick a third before bed Track for 7 days: How quickly can you shift your state?

Do you notice patterns?

Which technique works best for you?

Your vagus nerve is waiting Give it instructions. It is listening.

CHAPTER 6 , SLEEP, DREAMS, AND THE NIGHT SHIFT BRAIN

Here's the truth nobody wants to hear.

Everything else you're doing to heal your nervous system- all the breathwork, the vagal toning, the thought-reframing.

Will only get you halfway if you're not sleeping.

Sleep isn't rest. Sleep is repair.

It's when your brain takes out the trash.

Consolidates memories

Rewires neural pathways

Balances hormones

Heals tissue

Resets the nervous system Without sleep, you're running a system that's trying to clean itself with the lights still on

WHAT ACTUALLY HAPPENS WHEN YOU SLEEP

Most people think sleep is just... nothing.

Merely your body shutting down. Dead time.

Wrong Sleep is wildly active. Your brain is working harder during some stages of sleep than when you're awake.

The Sleep Architecture

Every night, you cycle through different stages. Each stage has a specific job.

Stage 1: Light Sleep (5-10 minutes)

Transition state

Muscles start to relax Brain waves slow down You can be easily woken Stage 2: Light Sleep (20 minutes)

Heart rate slows

Body temperature drops

Brain waves slow further with occasional bursts (sleep spindles)

Sleep spindles are linked to memory consolidation and learning A 2018 study from MIT found that people with more sleep spindles performed better on memory tasks Stage 3: Deep Sleep (20-40 minutes)

Also called Slow-Wave Sleep (SWS)

This is where the magic happens What happens in deep sleep: Growth hormone is released (repairs tissue, builds muscle)

Glymphatic system activates (brain's waste removal system)

Immune system strengthens

Memories are transferred from short-term to long-term storage Glucose metabolism is restored Adenosine (the sleepiness chemical) is cleared Without enough deep sleep: You feel foggy, even after 8 hours

Immune function drops

Blood sugar regulation suffers

You age faster

Stage 4: REM Sleep (10-60 minutes)

Rapid Eye Movement. This is where you dream vividly.

What happens in REM

Emotional processing and integration

Creative problem-solving

Procedural memory consolidation (skills, habits)

Neural pathway pruning (getting rid of what you don't need)

Neuroplasticity peaks

Dr. Matthew Walker, sleep scientist at UC Berkeley and author of Why We Sleep, calls REM "overnight therapy" It's when your brain processes emotional experiences and strips away the emotional charge.

That's why things often feel less overwhelming "after sleeping on it"

Your REM sleep literally soothed the emotional sting.

The cycle repeats 4-6 times per night.

Early cycles have more deep sleep.

Later cycles have more REM.

This is why

Cutting sleep short robs you of REM.

Sleeping but not deeply robs you of restoration. Both are disasters.

THE GLYMPHATIC SYSTEM: YOUR BRAIN'S NIGHT JANITOR

This is one of the most important discoveries in neuroscience in the last decade.

In 2012, Dr. Maiken Nedergaard at the University of Rochester discovered the glymphatic system

What it does

During deep sleep, your brain cells literally shrink by 60%. This creates space for cerebrospinal fluid to flush through and wash away toxic waste products.

What it removes

Beta-amyloid (associated with Alzheimer's)

Tau proteins (associated with dementia)

Metabolic waste

Cellular debris

Think of it as your brain's dishwasher It only runs at night And only during deep sleep A 2019 study from Boston University showed this process in real-time using brain scans.

They watched waves of cerebrospinal fluid pulsing through sleeping brains, washing away the day's accumulated junk.

Without enough deep sleep: The trash builds up

Year after year

And this is now understood to be a major factor in neurodegenerative diseases Chronic poor sleep increases risk of: Alzheimer's by 400% Dementia by 300% Cognitive decline by 200% Sleep isn't optional. It's vital for survival.

THE SLEEP-EMOTION CONNECTION

Ever notice how everything feels worse when you're tired?

That's not just perception. That's neurobiology.

The Amygdala Amplification Effect

In Dr. Matthew Walker studies using brain scans, he compared people who had a full night's sleep to those who were sleep-deprived. Then showed them emotionally negative images.

Results: Sleep-deprived brains showed 60% more amygdala reactivity.

And the connection between the amygdala and prefrontal cortex (the boss) was severed Translation: When you're tired, your emotional brain is screaming. And your rational brain can't calm it down.

The child and parent are in full control The boss has been locked out This is why minor annoyances feel like catastrophes when you haven't slept.

Why small stresses trigger massive reactions.

Why you cry over spilled coffee or snap at loved ones.

You're not nasty. You're sleep-deprived.

Sleep and Anxiety

A 2018 study from UC Berkeley found that just one night of poor sleep increased anxiety levels by an average of 30%.

Chronic insomnia increases anxiety disorder risk by: Generalized Anxiety Disorder: 270% Social Anxiety: 190% Panic Disorder: 340%

The vicious cycle

Anxiety disrupts sleep. Poor sleep increases anxiety which disrupts sleep more. The only way out is to break the cycle deliberately

THE CIRCADIAN RHYTHM: YOUR BODY'S MASTER CLOCK

You have a 24-hour biological clock.

Governed by a cluster of cells in your brain called the suprachiasmatic nucleus (SCN)

It controls

When you feel sleepy When you feel alert

Body temperature

Hormone release

Hunger signals

Immune function

The clock is set by: 1. Light (primary cue)

2. Food timing 3. Social rhythms 4. Temperature

The Light Problem

Your SCN is directly connected to your eyes.

When light hits your retina, it signals: Daytime! Be alert!

Blue light (from screens) is especially powerful. It mimics sunlight and tells your brain it's noon even if it's midnight.

What happens

Blue light suppresses melatonin (your sleep hormone) by up to 50% Studies have found that people who used screens before bed: Took 10 minutes longer to fall asleep Had 16% less REM sleep Felt groggier in the morning Had disrupted circadian rhythms for days after Your ancestors went to bed when the sun set.

You scroll Instagram until your eyes burn and wonder why you can't sleep.

The Cortisol-Melatonin Seesaw

Your body runs on two main hormones for sleep-wake cycles Cortisol (wake up hormone): Should peak in the morning Gradually decline through the day Be lowest at night Melatonin (sleep hormone): Should start rising at dusk Peak around 2-4 am.

Drop at dawn

When this rhythm is disrupted: You're wired at night You're exhausted in the morning You can't fall asleep You can't stay asleep You wake up feeling like garbage The modern assault on this rhythm: Screens at night (blue light)

Late caffeine

Irregular sleep times

Alcohol Stress (cortisol stays high when it should drop)

THE SLEEP DESTROYERS

Let's talk about what's actually ruining your sleep.

1. CAFFEINE (Half-Life: 6 Hours)

If you drink coffee at 4 pm, at 10 pm, half the caffeine is still in your system.

Caffeine blocks adenosine receptors.

Adenosine is the chemical that makes you sleepy. Blocking it is like putting tape over your "battery low" light.

The rule

No caffeine after 2 pm. Earlier if you're sensitive.

Caffeine consumed even 6 hours before bed reduces sleep by more than an hour.

2. ALCOHOL (The Sleep Thief)

Alcohol seems to help you fall asleep. But it destroys sleep quality.

What it does

Suppresses REM sleep (your emotional processing sleep)

Increases wakefulness in the second half of the night Disrupts breathing (increases snoring/sleep apnea)

Dehydrates you

Increases bathroom trips

Dr. Matthew Walker found that even one drink reduced REM sleep by 9% Two drinks reduced it by 24% You might "sleep" 8 hours, but your brain didn't rest.

3. SCREENS (Blue Light Hell)

We covered this, but it bears repeating.

Screens within 2 hours of bed directly suppress melatonin. But it's not just the light: The content matters too.

Watching news, scrolling social media, reading inflammatory content, all spike cortisol, activate your sympathetic nervous system. Tell your body: Danger! Stay alert!

Your ancient brain doesn't know the difference between:

A real tiger

A stressful work email A political argument online All of them feel like threats. All of them disrupt sleep.

4. LATE EXERCISE

Exercise is great for sleep. But not within 2-3 hours of bedtime.

Intense exercise

Raises core body temperature (you need it to drop to sleep)

Increases cortisol and adrenaline Activates the sympathetic nervous system Gentle movement is fine (yoga, stretching, walking) But don't do CrossFit at 9 pm, and expect to sleep at 10pm.

5. TEMPERATURE (Too Hot or Too Cold)

Your body needs to drop 2-3 degrees Fahrenheit to fall asleep.

Ideal sleep temperature: 65-68°F (18-20°C)

Too hot = you can't initiate sleep Too cold = you wake up during the night There is evidence to show that people who slept in rooms above 70°F: Took 15 minutes longer to fall asleep Had 25% less deep sleep Woke up more frequently 6. STRESS (The Cortisol Spiral)

When you're stressed, cortisol stays elevated at night. Instead of dropping as it should.

High nighttime cortisol

Keeps you wired

Triggers racing thoughts

Makes you feel "tired but wired"

Disrupts deep sleep

Wakes you around 3-4 AM (cortisol surge)

This is why chronic stress guarantees bad sleep. And bad sleep guarantees more stress.

The only solution: break the cycle with deliberate practices.

THE SLEEP SANCTUARY: BUILDING YOUR ROUTINE

Here's how to reclaim your sleep, step by step.

THE 90-MINUTE WIND-DOWN

Sleep doesn't start when you get into bed It starts 90 minutes before 90 minutes before bed: Dim the lights (all of them)

Turn off screens (or use blue-light blockers)

Lower the temperature

Begin transitioning to calm activities What to do in this window: Read (paper books, not Kindles with backlight)

Journal Gentle stretching or yin yoga Take a warm bath (the temperature drop afterward signals sleep)

Meditate or breathe

Listen to calming music Talk with loved ones (calm conversation, not arguments)

What NOT to do

Work

Check email

Scroll social media

Watch intense TV (especially news, thrillers, horror)

Argue

Pay bills

Plan tomorrow

This window is sacred. Protect it like your life depends on it. Because your health does.

THE SLEEP HYGIENE CHECKLIST

✓ Consistent sleep time (within 30 minutes, every night)

✓ Consistent wake time (even on weekends , yes, even weekends)

✓ Dark room (blackout curtains or eye mask)

✓ Cool room (65-68°F)

✓ Quiet (white noise machine if needed)

✓ Comfortable bed (invest in this; you spend 1/3 of your life here)

✓ No screens 90 minutes before bed ✓ No caffeine after 2 PM ✓ No alcohol close to bedtime ✓ Morning sunlight (10-30 minutes within 1 hour of waking)

That last one is crucial „ Morning light sets your circadian clock telling your body when the day begins, which then sets up when the night should begin.

THE 4-7-8 BREATHING TECHNIQUE

Created by Dr. Andrew Weil Based on yogic breathing practices clinically shown to initiate sleep in minutes

The practice

1. Exhale completely through your mouth (whoosh sound)

2. Close your mouth, inhale quietly through nose for 4 counts 3. Hold breath for 7 counts 4. Exhale completely through mouth for 8 counts (whoosh)

5. Repeat cycle 4 times

Why this works

The long exhale activates the vagus nerve Holding breath builds slight CO2, which makes you drowsy The rhythm distracts from racing thoughts Repeated cycles shift you into parasympathetic mode 4-7-8 breathing reduces sleep latency (time to fall asleep) by an average of 22 minutes Do this in bed, lights off, ready to sleep.

THE BODY SCAN FOR SLEEP

Progressive relaxation, systematically releasing tension

Lie in bed

Starting at your toes, consciously relax each body part

The sequence

Toes → feet → ankles → calves → knees → thighs → hips → belly → chest → fingers → hands → wrists → forearms → elbows → upper arms → shoulders → neck → jaw → face → scalp Spend 5-10 seconds on each area: "My toes are heavy and warm."

"My feet are sinking into the bed."

"My calves are soft and relaxed."

Most people don't make it to their shoulders before falling asleep WHEN YOU WAKE AT 3 am.

The dreaded 3 AM wake-up. You were sleeping fine, then suddenly... wide awake!

Mind racing! Heart pounding!

What's happening

Cortisol surge (stress response heart pounding!)

Blood sugar drop (if you ate late or poorly)

Shallow breathing (shift out of deep sleep)

Rumination triggers the sympathetic nervous system

What NOT to do

Check your phone

Turn on bright lights

Start problem-solving

Get frustrated (stress makes it worse)

What TO do

1. Reset your breath 4-7-8 breathing, or just slow, deep belly breaths 2. Body scan Progressively relax from toes to head 3. Cognitive shuffle Think of random, boring things that have no emotional charge "Blue chair, yellow lamp, red car, green tree..."

Your brain can't problem-solve AND do this simultaneously. Eventually, it gives up and lets you sleep.

4. Get up briefly (only if you've been awake 20+ minutes)

Go to another room

Dim lighting only

Read something boring

Do gentle stretches

Return to bed when you feel sleepy The goal isn't to force sleep. It's to return to a state where sleep can happen.

DREAMS: YOUR OVERNIGHT THERAPY

REM sleep is when you dream, and dreams are not random nonsense.

Dreams are

Emotional processing

Memory consolidation

Creative problem-solving

Threat simulation (your brain practicing scenarios)

Integration of new experiences with old knowledge

The Emotional Regulation Function

Dr. Rosalind Cartwright, dream researcher, found that people who were allowed to dream after emotional experiences showed: Better mood the next day

Less emotional reactivity

More balanced perspective on the event People who were deprived of REM (woken every time they entered it) showed:

Increased anxiety

Emotional dysregulation

Intrusive thoughts

Worsening mood

Dreams are how your brain integrates difficult emotions. Without dreams, trauma doesn't process, pain doesn't fade, Resilience doesn't build.

PTSD and REM Disruption

This is why PTSD is so devastating.

People with PTSD often have REM sleep disruption. They enter REM, start processing the trauma. But it's so intense, they wake up, over and over.

So, the trauma never gets processed. It stays raw, the emotional charge never decreases Recent research shows that therapies that support REM sleep (like prazosin, a blood pressure medication) can significantly improve PTSD symptoms Not by changing the memory, but by allowing the brain to finally process it during sleep

HOW MUCH SLEEP DO YOU ACTUALLY NEED?

Most adults: 7-9 hours Teenagers: 8-10 hours Older adults: 7-8 hours But it's not just duration, It's quality.

You can "sleep" for 8 hours but wake up exhausted if: You never reached deep sleep

REM was fragmented

You woke frequently

Sleep apnea disrupted breathing Alcohol or medication interfered How to know if you're getting enough: You wake naturally without an alarm (on most days)

You feel refreshed within 15-30 minutes of waking You don't need caffeine to function You don't crash in the afternoon You don't feel irritable or foggy If you need an alarm, you're not sleeping enough. Or you're not sleeping well enough.

SLEEP TRACKING: SHOULD YOU?

Wearables (Oura Ring, WHOOP, Apple Watch, etc.) can track:

Total sleep time

Sleep stages (light, deep, REM)

Heart rate variability

Sleep disruptions

Pros:

Objective data

Helps identify patterns

Motivates better habits

Cons: Can create "orthosomnia" (obsession with perfect sleep)

Devices aren't always accurate Anxiety about sleep scores can worsen sleep

The middle path

Track for a few weeks to identify patterns, then stop obsessing over numbers.

Trust your body's signals more than a device.

THE SLEEP DEBT MYTH

You can't "catch up" on sleep over the weekend. Sleep debt accumulates, and chronic deprivation has lasting effects.

A 2019 study from Penn State found that people who slept only 6 hours per night for 2 weeks showed cognitive decline equivalent to: Two full nights of no sleep And they didn't even realize it. They rated themselves as "functioning fine", while objective tests showed massive impairment.

When You adapt to feeling terrible You forget what normal feels like

THE NON-NEGOTIABLE

Everything in this book, the breathwork, the neuroplasticity exercises, the vagal toning, All of it requires sleep to consolidate.

Without sleep

New neural pathways don't solidify

Emotional regulation fails

The glymphatic system doesn't clear toxins

Hormones stay dysregulated

Inflammation increases

Healing doesn't happen

Sleep is not optional. It's the foundation.

In the next chapter, we'll explore breath , the most immediate, powerful tool you have to shift your state in real time. Because calm isn't just something you think about. It's something you breathe.

PAUSE & PRACTICE: Your 7-Day Sleep Experiment For the next 7 days, commit to: Same bedtime (within 30 minutes)

Same wake time (even weekends)

90-minute wind-down routine No screens after 8 PM 4-7-8 breathing before sleep Track: What time you actually fall asleep How many times you wake How you feel in the morning (1-10 scale)

Energy levels throughout the day After 7 days, you'll have data, and you'll feel the difference.

Sleep is the reset button your nervous system has been begging for.

CHAPTER 7 , BREATH: THE MOST UNDERRATED SUPERPOWER

You've been breathing since the moment you were born. About 20,000 breaths a day.

Over 7 million breaths a year.

And most of them have been wrong.

Not "wrong" as in you're dying. But "wrong"

as in you're missing the single most powerful tool you have for regulating your nervous system.

Breath is the only function that is both automatic and voluntary. Your body breathes for you when you're not thinking about it. But you can also take control at any moment.

This makes breath the bridge between the conscious and unconscious mind, between the thinking brain and the ancient brain, between chaos and calm.

THE MECHANICS OF BREATHING

Let's start with what's actually happening The Primary Muscle: Your Diaphragm The diaphragm is a dome-shaped muscle that sits beneath your lungs. When you inhale, it contracts and flattens, creating negative pressure that draws air into your lungs.

When you exhale, it relaxes and rises, pushing air out. This is "belly breathing" or "diaphragmatic breathing"

But most people don't breathe this way. They breathe with their chest, using secondary muscles (neck, shoulders, chest) that were designed for emergency breathing, not every day breathing.

The problem

Chest breathing is shallow; it doesn't fully exchange oxygen. It keeps you in a low-grade stress state, and it signals to your nervous system: Something's wrong Research consistently shows that people who habitually chest-breathe have: 31% higher baseline anxiety 24% higher cortisol levels Lower heart rate variability More frequent panic attacks You're literally breathing as if you're being chased, all day, every day and that is doing you no good.

THE BREATH-BRAIN CONNECTION

Every breath you take sends information to your brain about your state.

Fast, shallow breathing → Danger signal →

Sympathetic activation

Slow, deep breathing → Safety signal →

Parasympathetic activation

The CO2 Factor Most people think breathing is about getting oxygen. But it's actually about regulating carbon dioxide (CO2)

When you hyperventilate (rapid, shallow breathing): You blow off too much CO2

Blood vessels constrict

Less oxygen actually reaches your brain and tissues You feel dizzy, anxious, tingly This triggers more panic

You breathe faster

Vicious cycle

When you breathe slowly: CO2 levels normalize

Blood vessels dilate

Oxygen delivery improves

pH balances

Nervous system calms

Dr. Konstantin Buteyko, a Ukrainian doctor, developed the Buteyko Method based on this principle. He found that slowing breath and increasing CO2 tolerance could reverse asthma, anxiety, and sleep disorders.

A review of the Buteyko Method has found: 70% reduction in asthma symptoms 90% reduction in rescue inhaler use Significant improvement in anxiety and sleep All from learning to breathe slower, and tolerate slightly higher CO2.

THE FOUR BREATHING PATTERNS

There are four basic ways humans breathe.

Each creates a different state.

1. SYMPATHETIC BREATHING (Fight-or-Flight)

Pattern: Fast, shallow, irregular, through the mouth Effects:

Heart rate increases

Blood pressure rises

Cortisol and adrenaline release

Pupils dilate

Digestion stops

Muscles tense

When it's useful: Actual emergencies, intense exercise When it's harmful: Chronic stress, anxiety, sitting at your desk all day Stats: Most people breathe an average of 15- 20 breaths per minute at rest. Optimal is 5-6 breaths per minute. We're breathing 3-4 times faster than we should be.

2. PARASYMPATHETIC BREATHING (Rest-and- Digest)

Pattern: Slow, deep, rhythmic, through the nose Effects:

Heart rate decreases

Blood pressure lowers

Vagus nerve activates

Digestion resumes

Muscles relax

Cortisol drops

When it's useful: Recovery, sleep, healing, learning, creativity. This should be your default state 3. COHERENT BREATHING (Balance)

Pattern: 5-6 breaths per minute (inhale 5 seconds, exhale 5 seconds)

Effects: Perfect balance between sympathetic and parasympathetic Maximizes heart rate variability Optimal for focus and calm alertness Coherent breathing for just 10 minutes: Increases HRV by 34% Reduces anxiety by 44% Improves attention and executive function When it's useful: Work, studying, before important events, anytime you need calm focus 4. BREATH HOLDS (Building CO2 Tolerance)

Pattern: Breathe in, hold, breathe out, hold Effects: Increases CO2 tolerance

Strengthens diaphragm

Improves oxygen utilization

Reduces breathlessness

Calms panic response
When it's useful: Managing anxiety, improving athletic performance, sleep apnea, asthma

THE BREATHING TECHNIQUES ARSENAL

Here are the most powerful breathing techniques, each with specific uses.

BOX BREATHING (For Focus & Calm)

Used by Navy SEALs before high-pressure missions

The pattern
Inhale for 4 counts Hold for 4 counts Exhale for 4 counts Hold for 4 counts Repeat for 5 minutes

What it does

Creates perfect balance
Anchors attention in the present

Interrupts rumination

Lowers heart rate
Activates prefrontal cortex (the boss)

A 2019 study with tactical operators found that box breathing before stressful missions: Improved decision-making by 26% Reduced physiological stress markers by 38% Increased feelings of control by 41% When to use: Before presentations, difficult conversations, high-pressure situations, when your mind won't stop racing ALTERNATE NOSTRIL BREATHING (For Balance)

Ancient yogic practice called Nadi Shodhana.

Modern science confirms it works.

The pattern

1. Close right nostril with right thumb 2. Inhale slowly through left nostril (4 counts)

3. Close both nostrils briefly (1-2 counts)

4. Release right nostril, exhale through right (4 counts)

5. Inhale through right nostril (4 counts)

6. Close both, switch 7. Exhale through left (4 counts)

8. Repeat for 5-10 minutes

What it does

Balances left and right hemispheres of the brain,

Synchronizes nervous system

Reduces anxiety and blood pressure Improves focus and mental clarity

The International Journal of Yoga findings

state that 10 minutes of alternate nostril breathing: Lowered blood pressure by 7 mmHg Reduced heart rate by 11 bpm Improved cognitive performance by 23% Balanced sympathetic/parasympathetic activity When to use: Before meditation, when feeling scattered, before sleep, when anxious 4-7-8 BREATHING (For Sleep & Anxiety)

Created by Dr. Andrew Weil, based on pranayama techniques. We covered this in the sleep chapter but it deserves emphasis.

The pattern

1. Exhale completely through mouth (whoosh sound)

2. Close mouth, inhale through nose (4 counts)

3. Hold breath (7 counts)

4. Exhale completely through mouth (8 counts)

5. Repeat 4 times

What it does

Acts as a natural tranquilizer

Forces slow breathing

Increases CO2 tolerance

Activates vagus nerve

Shifts brain waves toward relaxation When to use: Insomnia, panic attacks, before bed, when overwhelmed Warning: Some people feel lightheaded at first. Start with 4 breath cycles, build up to 8.

PHYSIOLOGICAL SIGH (For Immediate Calm)

Dr. Andrew Huberman's favorite. The fastest way to reduce stress in real-time.

The pattern

Double inhale through nose (big breath, then sip of air)

Long exhale through mouth That's it. One breath.

What it does

Fully inflates collapsed alveoli (air sacs in lungs)

Offloads maximum CO2 Directly stimulates vagus nerve Immediately shifts nervous system state Physiological sighs have been proven to reduce stress markers as effectively as five minutes of meditation When to use: Anytime, anywhere, instant reset Stuck in traffic, before responding to a difficult email, when you notice tension building WIM HOF METHOD (For Energy & Immune Boost)

Dutch extreme athlete Wim Hof developed this. Combines hyperventilation with breath holds and cold exposure. This is NOT for everyone.

The pattern

1. 30-40 deep breaths (fully in, relaxed out)

2. After last exhale, hold breath as long as comfortable 3. When you need to breathe, inhale fully and hold 15 seconds 4. Exhale and repeat 3-4 rounds

What it does

Temporarily alkalizes blood (lower CO2)

Releases adrenaline

Activates sympathetic system

Increases oxygen saturation

Followed by deep parasympathetic rebound

Boosts immune markers

A 2014 study in PNAS found that trained Wim

Hof practitioners could

Voluntarily activate their sympathetic nervous system

Suppress inflammatory response

Show 50% fewer flu-like symptoms when injected with endotoxin When to use: Morning energy boost, before cold exposure, immune support Warning: Never do this in water or while driving Can cause temporary loss of consciousness Work with trained instructor first COHERENT BREATHING (For HRV & Balance)

Simple but profound. 5.5 breaths per minute is the magic number

The pattern

Inhale for 5.5 seconds Exhale for 5.5 seconds Continue for 10-20 minutes

What it does

Synchronizes heart rhythm with breath Maximizes heart rate variability

Creates resonance frequency

Perfect balance between gas and brake pedals When to use: Daily meditation practice, during work for sustained focus BREATH OF FIRE (For Energy)

Kundalini yoga technique. Rapid, rhythmic breathing.

Advanced practice.

The pattern

Rapid, powerful exhales through the nose

Passive inhales

1-3 breaths per second 1-3 minutes

What it does

Energizes immediately

Clears mental fog

Activates core

Releases toxins

Warning: Can cause dizziness, not for pregnant women, people with high blood pressure, or heart conditions When to use: When you need a quick energy boost without caffeine

THE BREATHING MISTAKES YOU'RE PROBABLY MAKING

Mistake #1: Mouth Breathing Your nose is designed for breathing; your mouth is designed for eating.

Nose breathing

Filters air (removes 98% of particles)

Humidifies air

Warms air

Produces nitric oxide (dilates blood vessels, improves oxygen uptake)

Activates diaphragm naturally

Slows breath rate

Mouth breathing

Bypasses all filters

Dries out airways

Increases infection risk

Causes bad breath, dental problems Promotes shallow chest breathing Associated with anxiety and sleep apnea A 2020 study from Stanford found that chronic mouth breathers had: 43% more respiratory infections 37% more dental cavities 52% higher rates of anxiety Significantly worse sleep quality The fix: Tape your mouth at night (seriously)

Use specialized mouth tape or medical tape.

Forces nose breathing during sleep.

Start: Tape during the day while relaxing, build tolerance before sleeping with it.

Mistake #2: Chest Breathing Shoulders rising, chest expanding, neck tensing… That's emergency breathing The fix: Place one hand on chest, one on belly Breathe so only the belly hand moves.

Practice 5 minutes daily until it becomes automatic.

Mistake #3: Reverse Breathing Some people (especially anxious people)

breathe backwards. Belly pulls in on inhale, pushes out on exhale.

This creates maximum tension „ The fix: Lie on your back, place a small weight (book) on your belly, practice making it rise on inhale, fall on exhale.

Mistake #4: Breathing Too Fast Average person: 15-20 breaths per minute Optimal: 5-6 breaths per minute The fix: Set a timer. Gradually slow your breath over weeks. Your body will adapt Mistake #5: Never Holding Breath Modern people are afraid of breath holds.

They trigger panic.

But this creates CO2 intolerance, which creates more anxiety.

The fix: Practice gentle breath holds Start with 5 seconds after exhale

Gradually increase

Build CO2 tolerance

Reduce panic response

THE BREATHING ASSESSMENT

Let's measure your current breathing BOLT Score (Body Oxygen Level Test)

This measures your CO2 tolerance „

How to test

1. Sit quietly for 5 minutes 2. Breathe normally 3. After a normal exhale, pinch your nose 4. Start a timer 5. Wait until you feel the first urge to breathe (not maximum hold)

6. Stop timer

Your score

<10 seconds: Poor CO2 tolerance, likely anxious, poor sleep 10-20 seconds: Below average, room for improvement 20-30 seconds: Average 30-40 seconds: Good 40+ seconds: Excellent Correlation: Low BOLT scores are associated with: Anxiety and panic attacks Asthma and breathing disorders

Poor sleep

Chronic stress

Frequent sighing

Goal: Increase BOLT score to 40 seconds over several weeks of practice

Breathing Rate Assessment

Count your breaths for 1 minute at rest: 15-20+: Too fast, chronic stress state 10-14: Below average 8-10: Average 5-7: Optimal <5: Advanced practice (yogis, free divers)

THE 21-DAY BREATHING TRANSFORMATION

Here's a progressive protocol WEEK 1: Awareness & Foundation Day 1-3: Track breathing rate and BOLT score Day 4-7: Practice diaphragmatic breathing 5 minutes, 3x daily Goal: Shift from chest to belly breathing WEEK 2: Building Techniques Morning: Box breathing (5 minutes)

Midday: Coherent breathing (10 minutes)

Evening: 4-7-8 breathing (4 cycles)

Goal: Make slow breathing feel natural WEEK 3: Integration & Challenge Continue Week 2 protocol Add: Breath holds (build CO2 tolerance)

Use physiological sighs throughout day

Retest BOLT score

Goal: Breathing becomes automatic ally

Expected improvements

BOLT score increase of 5-10 seconds Breathing rate decrease of 3-5 breaths per minute

Reduced anxiety

Better sleep

More energy

Increased focus

BREATHING FOR SPECIFIC STATES

Need energy?

Wim Hof method

Breath of Fire

Box breathing

Need to calm down?

4-7-8 breathing

Coherent breathing

Long exhales (any pattern where exhale is longer than inhale)

Can't sleep?

4-7-8 breathing Coherent breathing with long exhales Body scan + slow breathing Panic attack?

Physiological sigh (immediately)

Then transition to 4-7-8 Or box breathing once calmer Need focus?

Box breathing

Coherent breathing

Alternate nostril breathing

Pre-performance?

Box breathing for calm focus Or Wim Hof for energized alertness

THE MOUTH TAPING REVOLUTION

This sounds weird. It looks weird. It works.

Dr. Mark Burhenne, a dentist and sleep specialist, found that mouth taping: Improved sleep quality by 30% Reduced snoring by 65%

Decreased morning grogginess

Improved oxygen saturation

Reduced anxiety

Why it works

Forces nose breathing

Which activates the diaphragm

Produces nitric oxide

Slows breath rate

Improves sleep architecture

How to start

1. Buy medical tape or specialized mouth tape 2. Start by taping during relaxation, not sleep 3. Once comfortable, tape before bed 4. If you wake panicked, remove tape 5. Most people adapt within 3-7 nights

Safety notes

Don't use if you have severe nasal congestion Don't use if you're sick with respiratory illness Remove immediately if you feel distress Not for young children

BREATHING AND LONGEVITY

Here's something I bet you didn't know.

Animals with slower breathing live longer Tortoises: 4-5 breaths per minute → lifespan 100-200 years Humans: 15-20 breaths per minute → lifespan 70-80 years Mice: 150-200 breaths per minute → lifespan 2-3 years Correlation doesn't equal causation, but the pattern is striking.

Studies on long-lived populations (Blue Zones) show: They tend to breathe slower Many practice breathwork or meditation

Lower stress markers

Better HRV

Slow breathing is associated with:

Lower inflammation

Better cardiovascular health

Stronger immune function

Slower cellular aging

Longer telomeres (protective caps on DNA)

You can't change your species, but you can change how you breathe.

THE BREATH AS ANCHOR

In meditation, the breath is often used as an "anchor" Something to return attention to.

Why breath?

It's always available

It's neutral (not emotionally charged)

You can't think about your breath AND ruminate simultaneously Observing breath naturally slows it Which automatically calms nervous system

The practice

Sit comfortably

Close eyes or soften gaze Simply notice the breath Don't change it, just watch When mind wanders (it will), return to breath

Continue 10-20 minutes This is Vipassana meditation. Mindfulness meditation. Breath awareness. Its known to help

Reduce anxiety

Reduce depression

Improve attention

Lower blood pressure

Increase gray matter in prefrontal cortex The breath teaches you: You can't control everything But you can influence one thing

And that's enough

Because that one thing shifts everything else

THE ULTIMATE BREATHING PROTOCOL

If I could only give you one breathing practice, it would be this:

MORNING:

5 minutes of coherent breathing (5.5 seconds in, 5.5 out)

Sets your nervous system for the day

THROUGHOUT THE DAY:

Use physiological sighs whenever you notice tension Check in with breath hourly Is it fast? Slow it.

Is it shallow? Deepen it.

BEFORE CHALLENGING MOMENTS:

Box breathing (2-5 minutes)

Calms and focuses

EVENING:

4-7-8 breathing (4 cycles) before bed

Signals sleep time

TOTAL TIME: 15-20 minutes daily ROI: Immeasurable

WHEN BREATHING ISN'T ENOUGH

Sometimes breathwork alone won't resolve anxiety and that's okay.

Breathwork is a tool, not a cure-all.

Seek professional help if: Breathing exercises trigger panic You have trauma around breathing (choking, drowning, etc.)

Anxiety is severe and persistent You have respiratory conditions (asthma, COPD, etc.)

Breathwork enhances other treatments.

It doesn't replace them.

In the next chapter, we'll get you moving , because your body has been trying to tell you something for years, and it's time you listened.

PAUSE & PRACTICE: Your Breath Baseline Right now, before reading further: 1. Count your breathing rate for 1 minute 2. Test your BOLT score 3. Notice: Are you chest breathing or belly breathing?

4. Notice: Are you breathing through your nose or mouth?

Write these down and then commit to: Week 1 protocol (diaphragmatic breathing practice)

Retest in 7 days Your breath is the most accessible tool you have. Learn to use it.

CHAPTER 8 , MOVEMENT: WHY YOUR BODY KNOWS WHAT YOUR MIND FORGOT

Your body is keeping a detailed record of everything that's ever happened to you.

That time you were humiliated in third grade The breakup that shattered you The accident you survived The chronic stress you've been carrying for years All of it lives in your tissues Not as memory. But as tension, pain, holding patterns, and restricted movement.

Your mind might have "moved on" but your body hasn't.

And until you teach your body to release what it's holding, your nervous system will keep running the same protective programs, over and over.

This chapter is about how movement isn't just exercise.

It's medicine

It's therapy

It's how you complete the stress cycle your body started but never finished.

THE BODY KEEPS THE SCORE

Dr. Bessel van der Kolk wrote an entire book with this title. And it's not metaphorical.

Trauma and stress get stored in the body.

In muscles, fascia, organs, nervous system.

Why This Happens

When you're threatened your body mobilizes massive energy to fight or flee.

Cortisol and adrenaline flood your system

Muscles tense

Heart races

You're ready to run or punch But in modern life you don't run or punch.

You freeze in the meeting. You nod and smile when you want to scream. You hold still during the medical procedure. You collapse inward after the rejection.

All that mobilized energy has nowhere to go, so, it stays locked in your system, creating chronic tension, pain, inflammation.

A 2019 study from Harvard Medical School found that people with chronic pain (with no structural cause) often had: History of unprocessed trauma or stress Elevated muscle tension in specific areas (corresponding to where they felt unsafe)

Restricted breathing patterns

Dysregulated nervous systems

The pain wasn't "in their head", it was in their body. Held as incomplete stress responses.

Somatic Memory

Dr. Peter Levine, who developed Somatic Experiencing therapy, explains it this way: "Animals in the wild rarely suffer from chronic stress or PTSD. Not because they don't face danger, but because they complete the stress cycle through movement"

A gazelle escapes a lion. Once safe, it shakes, tremors, then goes back to grazing.

The shake discharges the stress hormones.

Resets the nervous system.

Signals: Threat over. Return to baseline.

Humans don't do this

We hold

We suppress

We "power through"

And the body never gets the signal that the threat is over.

THE SCIENCE OF MOVEMENT AND THE NERVOUS SYSTEM

Movement is one of the fastest ways to shift your state and Here's why and how.

Movement Discharges Stress Hormones

Remember cortisol and adrenaline?

They're designed to mobilize you for action.

When you actually move you burn through them, complete the cycle and signal to your body: We did the thing. We escaped. We're safe now.

Just 20 minutes of moderate movement reduced cortisol levels by an average of 31% And this cortisol reduction is not over days.

It is immediate.

Movement Releases BDNF (Brain Fertilizer)

We mentioned BDNF in Chapter 3

Brain-Derived Neurotrophic Factor

It's like miracle-gro for your neurons Exercise is the most powerful BDNF releaser known A 2019 review in Cell Metabolism found that: Moderate exercise increased BDNF by 30% Intense exercise increased it by up to 200% This effect lasted for several hours post- exercise Regular exercise kept BDNF elevated chronically

What this means

After you move, your brain is primed for neuroplasticity. It's the perfect time to practice new thought patterns, learn new skills, rewire old programs.

Movement creates the biological conditions for change

Movement Activates the Vagus Nerve

Certain movements especially rhythmic, bilateral (both sides of body) movements, stimulate the vagus nerve.

Walking, swimming, dancing, drumming.

All create rhythmic patterns that calm the nervous system.

Studies have found that rhythmic bilateral movement: Increased vagal tone by 19%

Synchronized brain hemispheres

Reduced anxiety by 37%

Improved emotional regulation

This is why "taking a walk" helps when you're upset It's not just distraction, it's vagal activation.

Movement Shifts Brain Waves

Different types of movement create different brain states

Vigorous exercise

Increases beta waves (alert, focused)

Good for attention and problem-solving Rhythmic, meditative movement (yoga, tai chi, walking): Increases alpha waves (calm, relaxed awareness)

Good for stress reduction and creativity Very slow, mindful movement: Can increase theta waves (deep relaxation, insight)

Good for emotional processing and integration Research using EEG during yoga found: Significant increase in alpha waves Decrease in high-beta (anxiety-related)

waves Improved coherence between brain regions Your brain changes based on how you move

TYPES OF MOVEMENT FOR NERVOUS SYSTEM REGULATION

Not all movement is equal. Different types serve different purposes.

1. SHAKING AND TREMORING (For Trauma Release)

What it is

Voluntary shaking or allowing involuntary tremoring.

How to do it: Stand with knees slightly bent Start bouncing gently, then shake arms, legs, body Let it get wild if it wants to 5-15 minutes Or lie on back, knees bent, feet flat, let legs shake/tremor

Why it works

This is what animals do naturally. It discharges incomplete stress responses, releases stored tension.

Dr. David Berceli developed TRE (Trauma Release Exercises) based on this.

Studies on TRE found

48% reduction in PTSD symptoms 42% reduction in anxiety

Improved sleep quality

Increased sense of safety in the body When to use it: After stressful events, when feeling "wired,"

when noticing chronic tension.

2. WALKING (For Integration and Calm)

Why it's powerful

Bilateral (both sides moving)

Rhythmic Gets you outside (nature + sunlight bonus)

Easy to do

Low barrier to entry A 2018 Stanford study found that walking: Increased creative thinking by 60%

Reduced rumination

Improved mood

Lowered cortisol

Walking in nature (green space) was even more effective.

The University of Michigan study found: 20 minutes in nature lowered cortisol by 21% 30 minutes lowered it by 28% Diminishing returns after that (but still beneficial)

The practice

20-30 minutes daily, no phone, no headphones (at least sometimes).

Just you, your body, your breath.

3. YOGA (For Nervous System Balance)

Why it's powerful

Combines movement, breath, mindfulness.

Specific poses stimulate the vagus nerve.

It Builds interoception (awareness of internal states)

Yoga practitioners show

27% increase in GABA (calming neurotransmitter)

Improved mood

Reduced anxiety

Better vagal tone

More effective than walking alone for anxiety reduction.

Types of Yoga and their effects: Vinyasa/Flow: Energizing, focus, strength Yin/Restorative: Deep relaxation, parasympathetic activation Kundalini: Intense, transformative, nervous system reset Hatha: Balanced, foundational, accessible Key poses for vagal activation: Child's pose (compression on belly)

Cat-cow (spinal movement)

Legs up the wall (blood flow reversal)

Supported bridge (heart higher than head)

Corpse pose (complete surrender)

4. DANCE (For Joy and Emotional Release)

Why it's powerful

Combines movement, music, rhythm Activates reward centers (dopamine)

Social connection (if dancing with others)

Self-expression Fun (which is underrated as medicine)

Dance/movement therapy:

Reduces depression

Improves body image

Increases self-esteem

Enhances emotional regulation

Doesn't matter if you're "good" at it, put on music and move. 5 minutes. Notice how you feel after.

5. STRENGTH TRAINING (For Embodied Power)

Why it's powerful

Builds literal strength (counters feeling powerless)

Increases testosterone (confidence, drive)

Improves body image

Creates sense of competence Requires presence (hard to ruminate while lifting)

Resistance training

Reduces anxiety symptoms

Reduces depression by 23%

Improves self-efficacy

Better than cardio alone for mental health

The empowerment effect

Lifting heavy things teaches your nervous system: I am capable. I am strong. I can handle hard things.

6. TAI CHI / QIGONG (For Flow and Grounding)

Why it's powerful

Slow, deliberate movement Breath-synchronized

Meditative quality

Improves balance and proprioception Cultivates "qi" (life force energy, or in Western terms, optimized nervous system function)

Tai chi

Reduces anxiety

Improves sleep quality

Enhances immune function

Lowered blood pressure

Increased feelings of calm and centeredness Particularly effective for older adults, but beneficial at any age.

THE FASCIA CONNECTION

Fascia is the connective tissue that wraps around every muscle, organ, nerve, like a bodysuit under your skin.

And it holds memory.

When you're stressed or traumatized fascia tightens. Sometimes permanently.

Creating restrictions, pain, limited range of motion.

Myofascial Release

This is why deep tissue massage, foam rolling, and certain yoga poses feel so overwhelming sometimes, because, you're not just releasing physical tension , you're releasing stored emotional energy.

People receiving myofascial release often experience spontaneous emotional releases (crying, anger, laughter). These correlate with decreased pain and increased mobility These emotional releases complete unfinished stress responses.

This is why you might cry during a massage, or feel suddenly angry during hip openers in yoga. Your body is letting go of what it's been holding.

EXERCISE VS. MOVEMENT

Let's make a clear distinction here.

Exercise = structured, goal-oriented, often intense.

Movement = any form of physical activity, including gentle, playful, functional.

Both are valuable. But movement is more important for nervous system regulation.

The Problem with Exercise-Only Approach

If you're chronically stressed and you add intense exercise on top, you're adding more stress.

Your body doesn't know the difference between: Running from a lion Running on a treadmill at max heart rate Both look like threat. Both spike cortisol.

It has been found that people with high baseline stress who did only intense exercise: Had elevated cortisol that stayed high Showed signs of overtraining Actually increased anxiety over time But those who balanced intense exercise with gentle movement:

Lowered cortisol

Reduced anxiety

Improved recovery

The prescription

If you're wired: Gentle, slow, grounding movement If you're collapsed: More vigorous, energizing movement If you're balanced: Mix of both Listen to your nervous system, not your fitness app.

THE FREEZE RESPONSE AND MOVEMENT

Remember the three threat responses from Chapter 1? Fight, flight, freeze.

Most people with trauma or chronic stress are stuck in freeze.

Freeze looks like

Numbness

Disconnection from body

Inability to take action

Feeling stuck

Depression Dissociation Movement is how you thaw freeze.

But it has to be gentle, gradual. Forcing intense movement when you're in freeze can re-traumatize.

The Somatic Experiencing Approach

Dr. Peter Levine's method: 1. Titration , tiny amounts of activation at a time 2. Pendulation , moving between activation and calm 3. Completion , allowing the body to finish interrupted movements Example: If you froze during trauma, your body wanted to run but couldn't.

The practice

Imagine the situation (just briefly)

Notice any impulse to move Follow it slowly (maybe your legs want to push, your arms want to punch)

Do the movement in slow motion

Notice the relief

Return to calm
This completes the interrupted response.

Tells the nervous system: The threat is over. I did the thing. I'm safe now.

SITTING DISEASE: THE MODERN EPIDEMIC

The average person sits 9.3 hours per day.

More than they sleep.

Sitting is killing us, and dysregulating our nervous systems.

The Physiology of Sitting
When you sit for extended periods:

Blood flow slows
Lymphatic system stagnates (it needs movement to flow)

Hip flexors tighten (pulling body into defensive posture)

Diaphragm compresses (shallow breathing)

Glutes "turn off" (losing power and stability)

Spine compresses

Metabolism slows
Research has found that every hour of sitting increases: Anxiety risk by 14% Depression risk by 9% cardiovascular disease by 6% Mortality by 2% Even if you exercise, sitting 8-10 hours cancels out much of the benefit.

The Solution

Movement snacks
2-5 minutes of movement every 30-60 minutes.

Examples:

Stand and stretch

Walk around the room Do 10 squats

Shake your body

Roll your shoulders

Take 5 deep breaths with arms overhead People who take movement breaks every 30 minutes report: lower cortisol better mood

Increased productivity

Less back pain

Set a timer. Your body will thank you.

THE PLAY DEFICIT

Children move constantly. Running, jumping, climbing, wrestling, dancing.

It's not exercise. It's play. And it's how they regulate their nervous systems.

Adults have forgotten how to play. We "exercise" instead. Which is work.

The Neuroscience of Play

Dr. Stuart Brown, founder of the National Institute for Play, found that play: Activates the entire brain Releases endorphins and dopamine- Builds social bonds (oxytocin)

Increases resilience

Enhances creativity and problem-solving Play deprivation in childhood is correlated with:

Increased violence

Decreased empathy

Higher anxiety and depression

Worse stress management

Adult play deprivation leads to:

Chronic stress

Decreased joy

Relationship problems

Burnout

The practice

Do something physical just for fun.

No goals, no tracking, no optimization.

• Throw a frisbee • Jump in puddles • Dance like nobody's watching • Play tag with your kids • Go to a playground (yes, you)

• Do cartwheels • Wrestle with your dog If it feels silly, you're doing it right.

INTEROCEPTION: LISTENING TO YOUR BODY

Most people are exteroceptive i.e. focused outward on the world.

Few people are interoceptive i.e. tuned into internal body signals „ Interoception is crucial for nervous system regulation You need to know: Am I tense or relaxed?

Am I breathing shallow or deep?

Is my heart racing?

Where am I holding stress?

What does hunger feel like vs. anxiety?

Without interoception, you can't self-regulate.

You're flying blind.

Building Interoception Through Movement

Body scan during movement: While walking, stretching, or practicing yoga

Ask yourself

- What do I feel in my feet?
- Where is there tension?
- Where is there ease?
- What's my breath doing?
- What's my heart rate?

A 2000s-era study showed that consistent body-based practices significantly improve self-awareness and emotional balance.

Increased interoceptive awareness by 43%

Improved emotional regulation

Reduced anxiety

Enhanced decision-making (gut feelings became more accurate)

The more you listen to your body the better it can guide you

THE MINIMUM EFFECTIVE DOSE

How much movement do you actually need?

For physical health

150 minutes of moderate activity per week (WHO guidelines)

Or 75 minutes of vigorous activity Plus 2 days of strength training For nervous system regulation: 20-30 minutes of movement daily Mix of gentle and vigorous Movement snacks throughout the day One restorative practice per week (yoga, tai chi)

One play session per week More is not always better „ Especially if you're already stressed „ Listen to your body If movement makes you feel worse, you're doing the wrong type or too much.

MOVEMENT AND IDENTITY

Here's something subtle but powerful How you move shapes how you feel.

How you feel shapes who you think you are.

If you move through life hunched, tight, collapsed, you'll feel defeated, you'll identify as powerless.

If you move with openness, strength, fluidity, you'll feel capable, you'll identify as resilient.

This isn't "fake it till you make it." This is embodied cognition.

It is known that people who walked in a "depressed posture" (slouched, slow):

Felt more depressed

Had more negative thoughts Remembered more negative experiences Just from walking differently for 5 minutes, people who walked in an "uplifted posture"

(upright, springy):

Felt happier

Had more positive thoughts Remembered more positive experiences Your body teaches your brain who you are.

Choose movements that teach strength, not defeat.

YOUR MOVEMENT PRACTICE

Here's a simple daily practice that covers all bases Morning (10 minutes): Gentle stretching or yoga Some shaking to wake up 5 minutes of walking or dancing

Throughout day

Movement snacks every 30-60 minutes Notice and release tension Stand or walk during calls Evening (15-30 minutes): Something you enjoy (walk, yoga, dance, tai chi)

Slow, grounding

Ends with stillness

Once per week

Something vigorous (if your system can handle it)

Something playful

Something social (if possible)

Total time: 30-45 minutes daily, non- negotiable.

In the next chapter, we'll explore language , how the words you use literally shape your brain chemistry, and how speaking can be a form of vagal activation or dysregulation.

Because what you say to yourself matters more than you think.

PAUSE & PRACTICE: The Movement Check-In Right now, before you move on, Stand up.

Take 60 seconds to: Shake your whole body

Roll your shoulders

Twist your spine gently Stretch your arms overhead Touch your toes (or knees, whatever feels good)

Take 3 deep breaths Notice: How do you feel after just 60 seconds?

That's how easy this is. That's how fast it works.

Now imagine doing this multiple times every day for the rest of your life.

Your nervous system is begging you to move.

Stop making it wait.

CHAPTER 9 , THE LANGUAGE OF CALM:

WORDS THAT REWIRE (AND WORDS THAT DON'T)

Let me ask you something. What's the longest conversation you've ever had?

Was it with a friend? A partner? Your mother?

Wrong The longest conversation you've ever had is with yourself.

According to research, we have about 60,000- 80,000 thoughts per day. That's roughly 50- 60 thoughts per minute.

And here's the alarm. 80% of them are negative, 95% are repetitive.

Translation: You're basically playing the same dark playlist On repeat. In your head. Every day.

"I'm not good enough"

"I always mess things up"

"Why am I like this?"

"Everyone else has it together"

"I should be better by now"

Your brain can be a very mean roommate who never pays rent, and never shuts up.

WHY AFFIRMATIONS MAKE YOU FEEL WORSE

Okay, controversial opinion incoming Most affirmations are baloney.

There. I said it. Before you throw this book at me, hear me out.

You know those Instagram posts?

"I am abundant"

"I am a money magnet"

"I radiate confidence"

You say them while standing in your pajamas, eating cereal for dinner, wondering if you can afford next month's rent.

And your brain goes: "Yeah... no. We're lying. This feels terrible."

A 2009 study from the University of Waterloo (yes, someone finally studied this) found that: Positive affirmations made people with low self-esteem feel WORSE Why?

Because the gap between the affirmation and reality was too big. Their brain rejected it like a bad transplant.

If you're drowning in debt saying "I am abundant" Your brain knows its rubbish.

And it doubles down on the negative thoughts To protect you from delusion.

THE AFFIRMATIONS THAT ACTUALLY WORK

So, what does work?

Bridging statements

Affirmations that your brain can actually believe.

Instead of: "I am confident"

Try: "I'm learning to be more confident"

Instead of: "I am financially abundant"

Try: "I'm taking steps toward financial stability"

Instead of: "I never worry"

Try: "I'm getting better at managing my worry"

See the difference? One is a lie; one is a truthful direction.

Your brain accepts the second one because it's: 1. True (you ARE learning/getting better/taking steps)

2. Process-oriented (not demanding perfection)

3. Believable (doesn't trigger your internal BS detector)

I spent years saying "I am calm and peaceful"

While having panic attacks. Didn't work.

Now I say "I'm learning to calm my nervous system" My brain believes that because it's true.

YOUR BRAIN DOESN'T UNDERSTAND "NOT"

Remember the pink elephant problem from Chapter 2?

Tell someone "Don't think about a pink elephant" They immediately picture a pink elephant Your brain can't process negatives. It only processes the image.

"Don't panic" = your brain hears "PANIC"

"Don't fail" = your brain focuses on "FAIL"

"I'm not anxious" = your brain registers

"ANXIOUS"

This is why New Year's resolutions fail.

"I won't eat sugar" (Brain: sugar sugar sugar sugar)

"I won't be late anymore" (Brain: late late late late)

Your brain is like a very literal three-year-old, it only hears the noun.

The Reframe

Instead of: "I won't eat junk food"

Say: "I choose nourishing foods"

Instead of: "I won't be anxious today"

Say: "I'm practicing calm today"

Instead of: "Don't mess this up"

Say: "I'm going to handle this well"

Notice the shift? Tell your brain what *TO DO*, Not what *NOT to DO* Remember it as TO DO vs NOT TO DO.

In the brain, only TO DO registers. TO DO always wins.

I used to tell myself before presentations "Don't be nervous, don't forget your lines, don't bomb" Guess what happened? All of the above.

Now I say "I'm prepared. I'm present. I'm clear." (Still nervous, but I don't forget my lines)

THE POWER OF "YET"

One-word changes everything

"I can't do this" vs. "I can't do this yet"

Carol Dweck, Stanford psychologist, studied this. She calls it growth mindset vs. fixed mindset.

Fixed mindset: "I'm bad at math"

Growth mindset: "I'm not good at math yet"

That tiny word "yet"

Opens possibility, implies progress, removes permanence.

Her research with thousands of students showed: Kids taught to say “yet”: Persisted 40% longer on difficult tasks Improved scores over time Were less anxious about challenges Kids without “yet”:

Gave up quickly

Scores plateaued or declined Developed anxiety around difficulty Same kids. Different language. Different outcomes.

THIRD-PERSON SELF-TALK: TALK TO YOURSELF LIKE YOU’RE SOMEONE ELSE

This is going to sound weird but stick with me. Talking to yourself in third person is provenly effective.

Not “I can do this.” But “[Your name] can do this”

Not “I’m freaking out.” But “[Your name] is feeling anxious right now”

Dr. Ethan Kross at University of Michigan studied this (Yes, someone got a research grant to study talking to yourself, that’s how important it is)

What the good doctor found:

Third-person self-talk

Reduces emotional reactivity

Improves performance under pressure

Lowers cortisol

Activates prefrontal cortex (the boss)

Creates psychological distance from the problem

Why it works

When you say "I'm anxious" you're merged with the anxiety. You ARE the anxiety.

When you say "[Your name] is feeling anxious" You're observing the anxiety.

There's space between you and it.

I started doing this even though at first, I felt like a complete idiot. I started asking myself "Okay, you're stressed. What do you need?"

And you know what I found? I found that I listen to myself more when I talk to myself like I'm a person I truly care about.

Try it for one week, especially in stressful moments "[Name], you're okay. What's the one thing you can do or think right now to make yourself feel better than you are currently feeling?"

THE GRATITUDE THING (BUT NOT THE TOXIC POSITIVITY VERSION)

Full disclosure I used to roll my eyes at gratitude journals. The cynic in me scorned.

"Oh great, just be grateful for your trauma"

"Never mind your problems, think of starving children"

Till I learned - No. That's not what this is.

Real gratitude isn't toxic positivity. It's not denying your problems. It's training your brain to notice what's working, instead of keeping it fixated on what's not working.

Because of that negativity bias we talked earlier about. Your brain is like a heat-seeking missile for problems. It's trying to keep you safe by scanning for threats constantly.

But this makes you miserable Gratitude practice is basically about showing your brain the evidence that you're okay. That there is no threat.

The research is absurd: A 2015 study found that writing three things you're grateful for, Every day , For 21 days

Led to

23% reduction in cortisol

Increased serotonin production

Better sleep

Improved relationships

More optimism

Effects lasted for 6 months after stopping All these changes in your body just from writing three things a day for three weeks.

How To Not Make This Annoying

Don't write generic stuff like "I'm grateful for my family"

"I'm grateful for my health"

(Your brain tunes that out like elevator music)

Be specific

"I'm grateful my friend texted me exactly when I needed it"

"I'm grateful my coffee was perfect this morning"

"I'm grateful my dog didn't throw up on my laptop today"

(Yes, that last one was mine. It was a good day.)

Keep the gratitude small, specific, true.

Even on terrible days, especially on terrible days "Today was garbage, but the sunset was beautiful" „ "I'm grateful I cried, I needed that"

"I'm grateful I didn't punch anyone"

(Bar's low, but hey, progress)

COMPLAINING: THE HABIT THAT'S POISONING YOU

Quick question: How many times have you complained today?

Out loud? In your head? In text messages?

On social media?

Probably more than you think Research shows the average person complains 15-30 times per day "Traffic sucks" "It's too hot" "This coffee is terrible" "I'm so tired" "Why is this taking so long"

Complaining is like second-hand smoke for your nervous system.

Every time you complain your brain releases cortisol. Your neural pathways strengthen the "victim" pattern, your amygdala gets more sensitive.

You're literally training your brain to look for problems.

The Complaint Cleanse

Try this experiment. One week. No complaining.

Not out loud, not in your head, not to yourself.

Sounds impossible, right? First day I tried this I became immediately aware of how much I complain about everything, The weather, the traffic, my hair, other people's driving, how long things take, how expensive things are...

It was exhausting catching myself complaining.

But by day 4? I felt lighter, less irritated, more creative And by day 7? My baseline mood had shifted.

The rule: If something's worth complaining about, either fix it or accept it. But don't just marinate in it.

(Traffic sucks? Leave earlier or put on a podcast you love)

(Weather sucks? Change what you can control: your clothes, your plans)

(Person annoying you? Have a conversation or create distance)

Its all entirely up to you.

THE STORIES YOU TELL BECOME THE LIFE YOU LIVE

Every time you tell a story about yourself you're programming your brain: "I'm terrible with money" (Your brain: "Got it.

Make bad financial decisions.")

"I'm so bad at relationships" (Your brain: "Roger that. Sabotage incoming.")

"I'm always anxious in social situations" (Your brain: "Yes, ma'am. Initiating panic protocols.")

You're the author of your own story. Stop writing tragedy.

Story Editing

Instead of: "I'm terrible with money"

Try: "I'm learning to manage money better"

Instead of: "I'm so bad at relationships"

Try: "My past relationships taught me what I need"

Instead of: "I'm always anxious socially"

Try: "Social situations are challenging for me, and I'm working on it"

Notice I'm not asking you to lie, I'm saying reframe toward possibility.

A 2016 study on narrative therapy found: People who "rewrote" their personal stories Not denying the hard parts but rather changing the interpretation showed: 38% reduction in depression 42% increase in resilience

Better coping strategies

More optimistic outlook

Same facts. Different self-talk. Different life.

JOURNALING: CHEAPER THAN THERAPY

I know, I know "Keep a journal" everyone says it. They are right. And there's a reason it works.

Dr. James Pennebaker studied "expressive writing" for 40 years. His protocol: Write about your deepest thoughts and feelings, about an emotional experience. For 15 minutes for 4 days.

Results across hundreds of studies: „

Improved immune function

Fewer doctor visits

Better mood

Reduced anxiety and depression

Improved sleep

Better grades (in students)

Faster wound healing (yes, really)

Just from writing for 15 minutes.

The Types of Journaling That Work

Brain Dump

Just vomit everything onto paper. No editing, no grammar, no one will see it.

Get it OUT of your head and ONTO the page.

Gratitude Journaling

We covered this. Three specific things. Daily.

Future Self Journaling

Write from your future self-one year from now. What did you accomplish? Who did you become? What's different?

(This is crazy because your brain starts problem-solving toward that vision)

Worry Journaling

Anxious thoughts spinning? Write them down. All of them. Then close the notebook.

Research shows this "contains" the worry, gets it out of your head, reduces rumination by 37%)

I do all of these. Different ones for different needs, sometimes just two sentences "Today was hard. I'm still here."

That counts

THE WORDS THAT LOWER CORTISOL

Some words/phrases actually calm your nervous system. Use them deliberately.

"I'm safe right now"

(Tells amygdala to stand down)

"This is temporary"

(Removes catastrophizing)

"I can handle this"

(Activates prefrontal cortex)

"What do I need right now?"

(Shifts from panic to problem-solving)

"I'm doing my best"

(Self-compassion activation)

"This feeling will pass"

(Creates space from emotion)

"What's one thing I can do?"

(Breaks overwhelm into action)

I have these written on my bathroom mirror so I see them daily. Especially on the days I don't believe them.

THE LANGUAGE OF SELF-COMPASSION

Here's a radical idea: Talk to yourself like you'd talk to a friend.

Would you tell your friend "You're so stupid"

"You always mess everything up" "Why can't you just be normal?"

No? Then why do you say it to yourself?

Dr. Kristin Neff researches self-compassion Her findings: People with high self- compassion have: Less anxiety and depression

More resilience

Better relationships

Less perfectionism

More motivation (not less!)

Better physical health

Self-compassion isn't self-pity. It's treating yourself like a person deserving of kindness.

The Self-Compassion Break

When you're struggling say these three things: 1. "This is hard right now"

(Acknowledging reality)

2. "Other people feel this way too"

(Common humanity, you're not alone)

3. "May I be kind to myself in this moment" (Self-compassion)

That's it. Not fixing. Not solving. Just acknowledging.

It doesn't fix the problem. But it changes how you are dealing with the problem.

SPEAKING YOUR TRUTH: THE VAGAL ACTIVATION OF HONESTY

Here's something fascinating: When you lie or withhold truth , Your vagus nerve knows.

Dishonesty (even white lies), even not saying what you need to say activates your stress response.

That tight throat feeling? That's your vagus nerve. "Hey! Something's not aligned here!"

Speaking your truth „ (Even when it's uncomfortable) activates the ventral vagal, reduces cortisol, creates authenticity.

A 2015 study at Notre Dame found people who lied less: Had better mental health

Better physical health

Better relationships

Less stress

Not the "be brutally honest about everything"

kind of truth, but "stop betraying yourself by staying silent" kind of clarity.

How many times have you: Said yes when you meant no Agreed when you disagreed Laughed when something hurt Stayed quiet when you wanted to speak Each time, your body kept score I'm not saying blow up every relationship with "radical honesty" I'm just saying stop lying to yourself about what you actually feel and need.

THE UPGRADE: CHANGING YOUR INTERNAL LANGUAGE

Your mental chatter is a habit. Like biting your nails or checking your phone.

You can change it. But before you can change it you have to first notice it.

Week 1: Just Notice Don't try to change anything, just become aware. What's your most common thought?

Write it down. That one thought you repeat most.

Week 2: Challenge It Is it true? Is it helpful? Is it serving me?

Would you say it to a friend or someone you cared about?

Usually the answers are: No, no, and hell no!

Week 3: Replace It Not with a lie but with a better truth.

"I should be better" → "I'm learning and growing"

"I always fail" → "I've succeeded before and I will again"

"Nobody likes me" → "Some people appreciate me"

Week 4: Practice Your brain will default to the old pattern, that's normal. Just keep redirecting it.

Like training a puppy , "Nope, not that thought" "Try this one instead"

SILENCE: THE MOST POWERFUL LANGUAGE

Sometimes the most powerful thing you can say is nothing. That's not suppression. It is strategic silence. You don't have to respond to every criticism, question, provocation, or opinion.

Silence is a complete sentence.

Sometimes not responding IS the best response. Remember that for yourself and remember it for others too. If someone goes silent, respect it. Don't chase. Move on.

Next: We're entering the war zone , your relationship with technology. Because your phone is literally hijacking your nervous system, and it's time to take it back.

PAUSE & PRACTICE: The Language Audit For the next 24 hours track your self-talk Every time you notice a thought about yourself, write it down.

At the end of 24 hours read what you wrote.

Would you say these things to someone you love?

If the answer is no, it's time for new language.

Choose ONE negative thought pattern.

Replace it with a bridging statement. Practice for 7 days.

Your brain is listening and responding to every signal you send it. Give it better data.

CHAPTER 10 , DIGITAL DETOX FOR THE ANCIENT BRAIN: YOUR PHONE IS NOT YOUR FRIEND

Let me guess. You picked up your phone today within 5 minutes of waking up? Or was it 5 seconds? Before your eyes were fully open, before your first conscious thought, before you even went to the bathroom. You checked your phone.

The average person checks their phone 96 times a day. That's once every 10 minutes.

While awake. Some studies say it's closer to 150 times. We are not using our phones.

We're being used by our phones.

YOUR ANCIENT BRAIN VS. THE ATTENTION ECONOMY

Here's the thing. Your brain evolved over millions of years. To scan for threats, to seek novelty, to crave social connection.

Tech companies know this, and they're weaponizing it.

Every app you use is designed by teams of engineers whose entire job is to hijack your nervous system.

That little red notification dot? The infinite scroll? The autoplay next video? The "someone liked your post"?

All deliberately engineered to trigger dopamine, keep you hooked, and pull you back into the app, often at the cost of awareness.

Sean Parker (Facebook's first president)

literally said: "We need to give you a little dopamine hit every once in a while. Because someone liked or commented on a photo or post. And that's going to get you to contribute more content."

They know what they're doing. This is intentional.

For them, it's business.

For you, it's attention, time, and nervous system bandwidth.

Is the exchange actually worth it?

THE DOPAMINE CASINO IN YOUR POCKET

Your phone is a slot machine. You pull to refresh (Like pulling a slot machine lever)

Sometimes there's a reward (New likes!

Messages! Drama!) Sometimes there isn't This is called variable ratio reinforcement It's the most addictive reward schedule known to psychology.

Casinos use it, social media uses it, your brain can't resist it.

A Stanford study found that social media notifications: Spike dopamine by 400% (that's FOUR

HUNDRED)

Activate the same brain regions as cocaine Create the same craving patterns as gambling addiction You're not weak. You're up against billion- dollar companies who hired neuroscientists to make their apps impossible to resist.

THE CORTISOL DRIP

But it's not just dopamine, it's cortisol too.

Every time you check your phone your amygdala scans for threat.

Bad news? Threat Someone mad at you? Threat Political argument? Threat Comparison to someone's perfect life? Threat A 2019 study tracked people's cortisol throughout the day. Cortisol spiked every time they checked social media, even when nothing was wrong. Just the act of checking.

Because your primitive brain doesn't know the difference between: A tiger in the grass

An angry email

Someone subposting you on Twitter All feel like danger. All trigger stress response. And unlike the tiger, these social media threats never end.

FOMO: FEAR OF MISSING OUT (WHILE MISSING YOUR ACTUAL LIFE)

The cruelest trick social media plays: Making you feel like you're connecting while actually isolating you.

You're scrolling through other people's highlights. Their vacations. Their perfect relationships. Their perfect looks. Their success. Their abs. Their buttocks.

And you're sitting in your pajamas, eating pizza, feeling like a failure.

A massive 2018 study from University of Pennsylvania: Participants limited social media to 30 minutes per day. For three weeks.

Results: 30% reduction in anxiety 20% reduction in depression 15% reduction in loneliness 18% reduction in FOMO From just limiting (not eliminating) social media to 30 minutes daily.

Think about that: what you're feeling might not be you at all, it might be Instagram!

THE COMPARISON TRAP

Social media is a highlight reel while you're comparing your behind-the-scenes to everyone else's curated performance.

Nobody posts

"Had anxiety attack in Target parking lot"

"Cried in the shower for 20 minutes"

"Fought with partner about loading the dishwasher"

"Feel like a fraud"

They post

Perfect breakfast

Beach vacation

Achievement unlocked

#Blessed Your brain sees this and thinks: "Everyone's life is better than mine"

"I'm the only one struggling"

"What's wrong with me?"

Nothing is wrong with you. You're merely comparing your reality to other people's performance art.

I once saw someone post a "candid" beach photo with the caption "Just living my best life!" I was there. I watched her take 47 versions of that "candid" shot while complaining the entire time about sand in her bathing suit.

Social media is fiction. Don't judge your life by someone else's creative writing.

NOTIFICATION CULTURE: TRAINING YOURSELF TO BE INTERRUPTED

How often is your focus actually uninterrupted? Researchers at UC Irvine found that the average person is interrupted or switches tasks every 3 minutes and 5 seconds. And it takes an average of 23 minutes to fully refocus.

Do the math. You're never actually focused.

Every notification is an interruption. Every buzz. Every ding. Every banner.

Your phone is training you to have the attention span of a goldfish.

A 2015 Microsoft study found: Human attention span in 2000: 12 seconds Human attention span in 2015: 8 seconds Goldfish attention span: 9 seconds The average human attention span is now shorter than a goldfish's.

No further notes.

Congratulations to us.

THE PHANTOM VIBRATION

You know that feeling when you swear your phone vibrated but it didn't?

That's called "phantom vibration syndrome"

And 80% of people experience it.

Your nervous system is so attuned to your phone that it hallucinates alerts.

This is not normal. This is addiction.

BREAKING UP WITH YOUR PHONE (SORT OF)

Look, I'm not going to tell you to throw your phone away. But there's a middle ground.

PHASE 1: AWARENESS (Week 1)

Track your usage without changing anything On iPhone: Screen Time On Android: Digital Wellbeing Just look at the numbers. No judgment.

Just reality.

When I first did this, I was spending 5.5 hours a day on my phone.

FIVE AND A HALF HOURS! That's a part-time job. A job where I get paid in cortisol and anxiety.

What's your number?

PHASE 2: BOUNDARIES (Week 2)

Turn off ALL non-essential notifications. Only keep on: Calls from actual humans Messages from real friends/family Turn off social media, news, email, games, and everything else.

Your phone should not interrupt you.

You should choose when to check it.

When I did this, I realized I had 47 apps sending notifications. FORTY-SEVEN.

I'm not that important. Neither are you (Sorry, but it's true) So why are you letting these apps do this to you?

PHASE 3: SACRED ZONES (Week 3)

Create phone-free zones/times: First hour after waking (Don't check your phone before you pee, meditate, or move)

Meals (Eat like a human, not a screen zombie)

Bedroom (Get a real alarm clock, yes, they still exist)

Conversations (If your phone is on the table, you're not actually present)

I bought an inexpensive alarm clock. Ugly as hell with bright red numbers. Kept my phone out of my bedroom My sleep improved 40% within one week.

PHASE 4: INTENTIONAL USE (Week 4)

Stop mindless scrolling, every phone session has a purpose.

"I'm going to check messages" Then only check messages. Nothing else. Then put phone down.

Not: "I'm checking messages" → Oh, Instagram notification → 40 minutes later → How did I end up watching a video about Shih Tzu's?

(Okay, Shih Tzu's are cute, but you get the point)

THE MORNING PHONE RULE: THE MOST IMPORTANT BOUNDARY

Never check your phone first thing in the morning. Why?

The first hour of your day sets your nervous system's baseline for the entire day.

If you wake up and immediately: Check news (cortisol)

Check social media (comparison, dopamine hit)

Check email (stress about work)

Check messages (other people's needs before yours)

You've started your day in reactive mode responding to external demands, before you've even brushed your teeth.

Research has found that people who checked phones within 5 minutes of waking: Had 27% higher cortisol all day Reported 32% more stress Were 40% more likely to feel overwhelmed Had worse mood regulation People who waited at least one hour:

Lower baseline cortisol

Better mood

More sense of control

Higher productivity

One hour. That's it. Wake up. Stretch, breathe, move, shower, eat, meditate. Whatever your body needs give it. THEN check your phone.

I fought this for months "But what if something important happened?"

Nothing important happens at 6 AM That can't wait until 7 AM (Unless you're a doctor on call, then ignore this)

SOCIAL MEDIA: THE NUANCED APPROACH

I'm not going to tell you to delete all social media. Some of it actually serves you. The question is: Which parts?

The Audit

Go through every app, ask yourself: Does this make me feel good?

Does this add value to my life?

Do I learn something useful?

Do I genuinely enjoy this?

Or: Does this make me feel bad about myself?

Do I feel worse after using it?

Is this just habit/addiction?

Am I comparing myself constantly?

Keep what serves you

Delete what doesn't

The People Audit

Unfollow/mute people who make you feel bad I don't care if it's:

Your cousin

Your high school friend That influencer everyone loves Someone you feel obligated to follow If their posts make you feel worse , Unfollow. You're not being mean.

You're protecting your nervous system.

I unfollowed 200 people last year including some I actually like in real life. But their online presence was toxic for me My anxiety dropped significantly after I did this.

Your feed is your mental diet. Curate it carefully.

THE PHONE BASKET: SOCIAL GATHERINGS

Here's a radical idea. When you have people over -everyone puts their phones in a basket.

First person to insist on having their phone back before the dinner ends, pays for dessert/next dinner. Compulsory. No excuses.

I started doing this with friends. First time was awkward, very awkward. I was sure I would lose many friends. People literally twitched, avoided eye contact.

But then? We actually talked, made eye contact, told stories, laughed...

Afterward, everyone said "That was the best dinner we've had in months"

Because we were actually present for each other, not distracted by our screens.

THE COST OF CONSTANT CONNECTIVITY

Being always available is killing you Your brain never gets to rest. Never gets to process. Never gets to just BE.

Before smartphones

You were bored sometimes, waiting in line, sitting in traffic, relaxing between tasks...

Boredom is when your brain processes.

Makes connections. Gets creative. Rests.

Now? There is no boredom. Every spare second you are scrolling. Your brain is in a state of constant overstimulation. Your brain is exhausted.

A 2019 study on boredom found: People who allowed themselves to be bored for 15 minutes daily: Had significantly more creative insights

Better problem-solving abilities

Lower anxiety

Better focus

Boredom isn't the enemy. Constant over stimulation is.

THE WEEKEND DIGITAL DETOX

Once a month go 24 hours with no phone.

Saturday morning to Sunday morning keep your phone off or left at home.

"But what if there's an emergency?"

There won't be. And if there is, people managed for thousands of years without cell phones, you'll survive 24 hours. For immediately family leave an emergency contact number if required.

I was terrified the first time. Genuinely anxious. Within 3 hours I felt lighter. Like I'd put down a heavy bag I didn't know I was carrying.

By hour 12: I'd read a book, had an actual conversation with my family, taken a walk and noticed trees By hour 24: I didn't want to turn my phone back on.

Now I do this monthly. Best thing I've ever done for my nervous system.

DIGITAL MINIMALISM: THE LONG GAME

Cal Newport wrote a book called Digital Minimalism. The premise: Most people have a maximalist relationship with technology , use everything, all the time, for every reason.

Minimalism means: , Intentional use, purpose-driven, not default behavior.

Ask yourself: What technology genuinely improves my life? What's just noise?

For me

Keep: Music streaming, maps, banking, calendar, reading apps Lost: Most social media, news apps, random games, shopping apps My phone now serves me instead of me serving it.

THE HARD TRUTH

Your phone isn't making you happier, more connected, more informed, more productive.

It's making you: More anxious, more distracted, more depressed, more reactive, more exhausted.

You know this but you keep scrolling. Why?

Because it's designed to be addictive.

And you're human. And humans are vulnerable to these exploits.

But you can choose differently.

THE 30-DAY PHONE RESET

Week 1: Track and observe Week 2: Turn off all non-essential notifications Week 3: Create sacred phone-free zones/times Week 4: Audit apps and people, delete/unfollow ruthlessly Then: Reassess How do you feel? Less anxious? More present? Better sleep? More time?

I guarantee you'll notice a difference.

Next: We're diving into relationships , because other people's nervous systems affect yours, and it's time to learn how to co-regulate without losing yourself.

PAUSE & PRACTICE: The Phone Drawer Challenge Tonight, put your phone in a drawer before bed.

Tomorrow morning, don't open the drawer for one hour after waking.

Do this for 7 days.

Track: How you feel in the morning Your anxiety level throughout the day

Your sleep quality

Your stress response

I'm betting: You'll feel significantly better, and you won't want to stop.

Your nervous system is begging for this.

Give it one week

CHAPTER 11 , RELATIONSHIPS AND THE NERVOUS SYSTEM: OTHER PEOPLE'S CHAOS ISN'T YOURS TO CARRY

Here's something nobody tells you about relationships: You don't just share space with someone; you share nervous systems.

That anxious person sitting next to you?

Your body feels it.

That calm friend who always makes you feel better? That's nervous system regulation We're not separate islands. We're interconnected physiological networks, broadcasting our internal state all the time.

And some people? Are broadcasting static.

CO-REGULATION: THE SUPERPOWER YOU DIDN'T KNOW YOU HAD

When you're around a calm person: your heart rate slows, your breath deepens, your cortisol drops.

You didn't decide this, it just happened.

This is called co-regulation and it's happening constantly.

The science: Your autonomic nervous system picks up cues from others.

Through:

Tone of voice

Facial expressions

Body language

Proximity- Even smell (pheromones)

Dr. Stephen Porges calls this "neuroception"

Your body reading safety or danger from other people's bodies without conscious thought.

A 2018 study at University of Virginia put couples in MRI machines and applied painful stimulus to one partner. The other partner's brain lit up in the same pain centers.

Not "I feel bad for you" but "I feel your pain in my body"

You are literally wired to feel other people

THE EMPATHY TRAP

Here's where it gets tricky. Some people are nervous system vampires. Not on purpose (usually), But they are so dysregulated that being around them feels like carrying their chaos.

You know the type: After 30 minutes with them: You feel drained anxious, irritable, exhausted. Your body absorbed their stress.

I have an aunt who I love dearly. But 10 minutes in her presence and my shoulders are at my ears, my jaw is clenched and my stomach is in knots. She's not doing anything to me specifically but her nervous system is just in such a perpetual alarm mode that mine responds.

This isn't lack of boundaries, it is biology

ATTACHMENT STYLES: THE NERVOUS SYSTEM OPERATING MANUAL FOR RELATIONSHIPS

Dr. John Bowlby and Dr. Mary Ainsworth discovered how your childhood shapes your nervous system's default mode in relationships.

There are four attachment styles: 1.SECURE ATTACHMENT (About 50% of people)

What it looks like: "I'm okay on my own, and I'm good with closeness".

Can handle conflict without freaking out.

Can be vulnerable without falling apart.

Can ask for what they need.

Can give space without fear.

Nervous system state: Ventral vagal (social engagement)

Origin: Caregivers were consistently responsive 2.ANXIOUS ATTACHMENT (About 20%)

What it looks like: "Please don't leave me, also you're probably going to leave me"

Hypervigilant to signs of rejection.

Needs constant reassurance.

Fears abandonment.

Clingy but convinced they're not wanted.

Nervous system state: Sympathetic activation (high alert)

Origin: Inconsistent caregiving (sometimes there, sometimes not)

3.AVOIDANT ATTACHMENT (About 25%)

What it looks like: "I don't need anyone, intimacy is uncomfortable"

Pulls away when things get close.

Values independence extremely.

Feels suffocated by emotional needs.

Dismisses their own emotions and others'.

Nervous system state: Shutdown (dorsal vagal)

Origin: Caregivers were dismissive or rejected emotional needs.

4.DISORGANIZED ATTACHMENT (About 5%)

What it looks like: "Come here! No, go away! Wait, don't leave!"

Wants closeness but fears it.

Unpredictable responses, trauma history.

Nervous system state: Oscillates between all states.

Origin: Frightening or frightened caregivers (abuse, trauma, addiction, violence)

WHY YOU KEEP CHOOSING THE SAME TERRIBLE PERSON

Here's the annoying truth: your nervous system seeks the familiar, even when the familiar is painful.

Anxious attachment + Avoidant attachment = Hell.

But also = Chemistry.

The anxious person: "Please love me!"

The avoidant person: "I need space!"

The anxious person: panics and pursues more The avoidant person: pulls further away This is called the anxious-avoidant trap.

Why do people stay in this torture?

Because to the anxious person the avoidant person's distance feels like home.

(Mom/Dad was inconsistent, remember?)

And to the avoidant person the anxious person's neediness confirms their belief "See? Intimacy is suffocating"

Both are getting their childhood beliefs confirmed which feels safe even though it's miserable.

A 2019 study found: People with insecure attachment consistently choose partners who reinforce their attachment wounds.

Not consciously. But their nervous system recognizes the pattern and goes "Yes! This is familiar! This is safety!"

(Your nervous system is an idiot sometimes)

EARNED SECURE ATTACHMENT: YOU'RE NOT DOOMED

Good news: You can change your attachment style. It's called "earned secure attachment"

Through: Therapy (especially EMDR or somatic therapy)

Secure relationships (friends, partners, mentors)

Nervous system regulation practices (everything in this book)

Self-awareness and intentional rewiring Research shows about 20-30% of people change their attachment style over their lifetime. It takes work but it's possible.

I'm still anxious attachment. But now I'm aware anxious attachment.

The difference

Before: "He didn't text back for two hours,

IT'S OVER"

Now: "He didn't text back, my anxious attachment is activated, this is a pattern, breathe, he's probably just busy"

I still feel it but I don't let it drive my car.

BOUNDARIES: THE NERVOUS SYSTEM SAFETY NET

Boundaries are not walls, they are information.

"I can't talk about this right now"

"I need space to process"

"That doesn't work for me"

"I'm not available for that"

Boundaries tell your nervous system: "You're allowed to have needs"

"You don't have to carry other people's stuff"

"It's safe to say no"

People who struggle with boundaries usually have nervous systems that learned: "My needs don't matter"

"I have to make others comfortable"

"Saying no is dangerous"

This creates resentment, burnout, anxiety, codependency, chronic people-pleasing,

The Boundary Formula

"I feel X when Y happens. I need Z."

Examples: "I feel overwhelmed when you call late at night. I need to not answer calls after 9pm."

"I feel disrespected when you show up unannounced. I need you to text first."

"I feel drained after three hours together. I need to limit visits to two hours."

Notice: No blaming, no apologizing, just stating needs.

When you start setting boundaries you will probably feel terrible, guilty, selfish, mean.

Then you will notice something: The people who respect boundaries – they stay.

And your relationship improves.

The people who got mad with your boundaries? They were the ones benefiting from your lack of boundaries to begin with.

Good riddance.

TOXIC RELATIONSHIPS: WHEN TO WALK AWAY

Some relationships are not salvageable and that's okay.

Signs you're in a nervous-system damaging relationship:

Physical signs

Stomach problems when you see their name Tension headaches after interactions

Sleep problems

Fatigue that won't lift Getting sick more often

Emotional signs

Walking on eggshells constantly Feeling smaller/less yourself around them Chronic anxiety about their reactions Your good news feels unsafe to share You're always explaining yourself

Behavioral signs

You dread seeing them You need hours to recover after interactions You're constantly defending them to others You've lost friends/family over this person You feel relief when they cancel plans If you checked more than 3: Your nervous system is screaming. Listen to it.

Toxic relationships increase risk of: heart disease, high blood pressure, anxiety disorders, depression and brace yourself - early death!

That toxic relationship is literally killing you.

I know it's hard. But staying is harder for you.

THE FIVE-MINUTE RULE FOR DIFFICULT CONVERSATIONS

When you need to have a hard conversation: Regulate your nervous system first.

5 minutes before: Breathe (4-7-8 or box breathing)

Ground yourself (feet on floor, notice body)

Remind yourself of your intention

Release outcome attachment

During: Speak from "I" statements Stay in your body (notice when you dissociate)

Take breaks if needed Use the physiological sigh if you get activated After: Process with movement (walk, shake, dance)

Journal if needed

Don't text 47 people about it Give yourself credit for showing up Conversations don't always go how you want.

But at least you can show up regulated.

SOCIAL ANXIETY: YOUR NERVOUS SYSTEM THINKS PEOPLE ARE TIGERS

Social anxiety isn't shyness. It's your amygdala screaming "THESE PEOPLE ARE DANGEROUS!" Even when they're not.

What your nervous system is detecting: Potential rejection = threat Potential judgment = threat Potential humiliation = threat Being seen = vulnerable = threat Your body responds accordingly: Racing heart, sweating, shaking, mind going blank, wanting to flee.

Classic sympathetic activation

The Social Anxiety Protocol

Before social events

Don't caffeinate excessively (you're already wired)

Practice physiological sighs

Remind yourself: "I'm safe, this is just anxiety"

Have an exit strategy (so you feel less trapped)

During: Focus on one conversation at a time (not scanning the room)

Ask questions (gets you out of your head)

Notice your feet on the ground (grounding)

Take bathroom breaks to reset (physiological sigh in private)

After: Don't ruminate on every awkward moment Move your body (discharge the activation)

Acknowledge you did hard thing Remember: most people are too worried about themselves to notice your anxiety

Pro tip

Arrive early when there are fewer people.

Your nervous system can adjust gradually instead of walking into sensory overload.

EMPATHS: YOU'RE NOT MAGICAL, YOU'RE JUST OVERWHELMED

"I'm an empath"

Translation: "I have a sensitive nervous system"

You're not psychic, you are hypervigilant. You learned young to read the room, to track others' emotions, to predict danger, to keep yourself safe. This is a trauma response not a superpower.

Yes, you're sensitive. Yes, you pick up on things others miss. But it's exhausting and it's not your job to absorb everyone's feelings.

Empath Protection Protocol

Before going into groups: Set intention: "I'm observing, not absorbing"

Visualize a boundary (whatever works for you)

Ground in your body During: Notice when you're picking up others' emotions Breathe and return to your own body You can be compassionate without taking on their stuff After: Shake it off (literally)

Shower (water is grounding. Salt water is cleansing)

Journal what's yours vs. what's theirs Time alone to reset Remember you can care without carrying other people's burdens.

CONFLICT: NOT A THREAT, JUST INFORMATION

Most people treat conflict like a tiger.

Something to avoid at all costs. But healthy relationships have conflict. They just know how to repair.

Dr. John Gottman (relationship researcher)

found that it's not the conflict that matters, it's the repair.

The Four Horsemen (relationship killers): 1. Criticism ("You always..." / "You never...")

2. Contempt (sarcasm, mockery, disgust)

3. Defensiveness ("It's not my fault!")

4. Stonewalling (shutting down, silent treatment)

Replace with

1. Complaint without blame ("I feel X when

Y")

2. Respect (even when angry)

3. Taking responsibility ("You're right, I did that")

4. Self-soothing first ("I need 20 minutes, then I'll come back")

Conflict is just two nervous systems trying to communicate needs while in threat mode.

The goal isn't to avoid conflict but to state your point while regulated.

THE PEOPLE YOU NEED (AND THE ONES YOU DON'T)

Not all relationships serve you and that's okay to acknowledge.

Green-Light People (Keep These)

You feel better after seeing them They celebrate your wins They're honest but kind

They respect boundaries

They can handle your authenticity Being with them feels like exhaling Yellow-Light People (Proceed With Caution)

Sometimes good, sometimes draining Can be supportive but also critical

Relationships feel transactional

You're not quite yourself around them Limited doses are fine Red-Light People (Exit When Possible)

You feel worse after seeing them They minimize your feelings Boundaries are not respected

Everything's a competition

You can't be authentic Your nervous system screams "DANGER"

Do an audit and see who's in each category?

Then decide

More of green. Less of yellow. Remove the red.

Your nervous system will thank you.

LONELINESS VS. ALONE TIME: KNOWING THE DIFFERENCE

Loneliness = Your nervous system seeking connection and not finding it.

Alone time = Your nervous system resting and resetting.

Loneliness feels like

Aching, Disconnection, "Nobody gets me"

Desperate for contact but somehow can't reach out.

Alone time feels like: Relief, Spacious, Restorative, "I needed this"

Both are valid. Honor what you need.

Extroverts: Need people to regulate Introverts: Need alone time to regulate Most people: Need both in different doses The pandemic taught us we need each other more than we thought. We need each other in person. Not just digitally.

Next: Trauma , when the past won't let go, and how to finally put it down.

PAUSE & PRACTICE: The Relationship Nervous

System Audit

Make three lists

GREEN LIGHT: People who make you feel calm/good YELLOW LIGHT: People who are sometimes okay, sometimes draining.

RED LIGHT: People who consistently make you feel worse.

Then: Schedule more time with green.

Limit time with yellow. Create distance from red.

Watch your baseline anxiety drop.

CHAPTER 12 , WHEN TRAUMA WRITES THE CODE: UNDERSTANDING AND HEALING WHAT WON'T LET GO

Let's talk about the T-word , Trauma.

Everyone's got an opinion "That's not real trauma"

"Other people have it worse"

"Get over it already"

Here's the truth: Trauma isn't what happened to you. It's what happens inside you and what you carry as a result of what happened in the past.

Dr. Bessel van der Kolk says it perfectly: "Trauma is not the story of something that happened back then. But the current imprint of that pain, horror, and fear"

It's not the event; it is the stuck response.

BIG T VS. LITTLE T (AND WHY BOTH MATTER)

Big T Trauma: War, assault, abuse, accidents, natural disasters. The stuff everyone agrees is traumatic.

Little t trauma: Bullying, emotional neglect, divorce, medical procedures, chronic stress.

The stuff people minimize "It wasn't that bad"

But here's the thing: Your nervous system doesn't rank trauma on other people's scales It just responds as it must till you heal.

That time your dad forgot your birthday?

Little t

That time you got stitches at age 5 while being held down? Little t That time your teacher humiliated you in front of the class? Little t All of these may be little t's in other people's eyes but can create lasting nervous system dysregulation in some.

A 2019 study from Harvard confirms: People with multiple "little t" traumas, often showed the same PTSD symptoms, as people with "Big T" trauma Your body doesn't lie. If you're stuck, you're stuck. Regardless of whether others think you "should" be or not.

THE WINDOW OF TOLERANCE

Imagine your nervous system as a window.

Inside the window

You can think clearly Feel your feelings without being overwhelmed

Connect with others

Handle stress reasonably

This is your "window of tolerance" , Above the window: (Hyperarousal)

Anxiety Panic Rage Hypervigilance

Can't sit still

Overwhelmed Below the window: (Hypoarousal)

Depression Shutdown Numbness Dissociation Can't get out of bed Disconnected Trauma narrows your window.

Normal window: Wide enough to handle most of life's ups and downs Trauma window: Tiny. The smallest thing pushes you out.

Someone looks at you wrong → hyperarousal Bad news → shutdown Recovery = widening the window.

Not eliminating stress but increasing your capacity to stay regulated when stress hits.

FLASHBACKS: YOUR BRAIN THINKS IT'S HAPPENING AGAIN

Flashbacks are not just memories. They are more.

Regular memory: "I remember that scary thing that happened"

Past tense. You know it's over.

Flashback: "IT'S HAPPENING RIGHT NOW"

Present tense. Your body fully believes you're in danger right now.

Why this happens

During trauma your brain tries to create a memory. But the hippocampus (memory organizer) goes offline. So, the memory gets stored fragmented without a time stamp.

It's like saving a file without a date.

Your brain doesn't know it's old.

Triggers bring it back: Smell, sound, time of year, similar situation.

And suddenly: Heart racing, can't breathe, panic. Even though nothing is actually happening right now.

You're not crazy. Your memory system is stuck.

COMPLEX PTSD: IT'S NOT ONE EVENT, IT'S A THOUSAND

PTSD = One traumatic event Car crash, assault, disaster, divorce, death...

Complex PTSD (C-PTSD) = Chronic, repeated trauma

Childhood abuse

Domestic violence

Emotional neglect

War zone

Toxic relationships

The difference matters. A lot.

PTSD symptoms: Flashbacks, Nightmares, Hypervigilance, Avoidance.

C-PTSD adds: Difficulty regulating emotions, Negative self-concept ("I'm bad/broken/unlovable"), Relationship problems, Dissociation, Physical symptoms (chronic pain, illness), Difficulty trusting anyone.

C-PTSD isn't officially in the DSM yet, (Diagnostic and Statistical Manual of Mental Disorders) but researchers agree it exists.

And it's more common than you think.

If you grew up in a chaotic household with unpredictable caregivers , you might have C- PTSD. Even if nothing "big" happened.

EMOTIONAL FLASHBACKS: THE ONES NOBODY TALKS ABOUT

Not all flashbacks are visual.

Emotional flashback = Sudden overwhelming emotion that doesn't match current reality.

Example: Your partner says "We need to talk"

Suddenly you're flooded with terror out of proportion to the situation.

What's happening: Your nervous system recognized a pattern.

"We need to talk" = childhood punishment conversations
Emotion from age 7 just showed up.

In your 35-or 45- or 55-year-old body.

Pete Walker, C-PTSD expert, identified 13 steps to manage emotional flashbacks:

The short version

1. Say to yourself: "I'm having a flashback" (Names it, creates distance)

2. Remind yourself: "It's from the past, not happening now" (Reality check)

3. Breathe deeply (Vagus nerve activation)

4. Ground in present (Five senses, current surroundings)

5. Be kind to yourself (Not "Get over it,"

but "This makes sense")

6. This works. I use it all the time.

DISSOCIATION: WHEN YOU LEAVE YOUR BODY

Dissociation is a spectrum: Mild: Zoning out during boring meetings Driving somewhere and not remembering the drive "Wait, what did you just say?"

Moderate: Feeling disconnected from your body Watching yourself from outside "I'm here but not really here"

Severe: Large chunks of time missing Not recognizing yourself in mirror Completely leaving your body (DID - Dissociative Identity Disorder)

Dissociation during trauma is protective If you can't escape physically, you escape mentally. But if it becomes your default it's a problem.

Signs you dissociate regularly:

Lose time frequently

Feel "floaty" or disconnected Watch yourself from outside your body Can't remember chunks of conversations Feel like you're in a dream

Chronic numbness

If this is you, you need professional help.

Specifically trauma therapy. Don't try to heal this alone.

THERAPIES THAT ACTUALLY WORK FOR TRAUMA

Not all therapy is created equal and talk therapy alone often isn't enough.

EMDR (Eye Movement Desensitization and Reprocessing)

What it is

You recall traumatic memory While doing bilateral stimulation (Eye movements, tapping, sounds)

Sounds weird but works incredibly well.

How? The bilateral stimulation helps the brain reprocess the stuck memory. Add the time stamp it was missing. Move it from "happening now" to "happened then"

Research: 84-90% improvement in PTSD symptoms often in 3-12 sessions.

I did EMDR for childhood stuff I thought I'd "dealt with." It changed my life. That memory that used to make my heart race? Now it's just... a memory. Neutral. Filed away properly.

Somatic Experiencing (SE)

Created by Peter Levine

Focus: Completing the body's interrupted stress response Remember the gazelle? Shaking off the lion chase?

This therapy helps you do that Through:

Tracking body sensations

Releasing held tension

Allowing tremoring/shaking Gradually discharging stuck activation Not talking about the trauma but letting the body process it and shake it off.

Especially good for

Pre-verbal trauma, somatic symptoms, people who don't want to talk about it.

Internal Family Systems (IFS)

The "parts" therapy Premise: You have different parts of yourself all trying to protect you.

The Anxious Part, the Angry Part, the Shutdown Part, the People-Pleasing Part.

They're all trying to help in their own misguided ways.

IFS helps you

Understand each part's purpose Appreciate what they're trying to do

Update their strategies

Integrate them into your "Self" (the wise, calm center)

This one blew my mind because it makes so much sense.

That voice in your head saying "You're not good enough"? That's a part probably trying to protect you from disappointment or failure. Once you understand that you can thank it and ask it to step back.

Neurofeedback: Training your brain waves.

You wear sensors, watch a screen.

When your brain produces calm waves you get rewarded. Over time your brain learns to produce more calm states.

Research shows

60-80% improvement in PTSD 40-60% improvement in anxiety

Often permanent changes

Downside: Expensive

Not widely available

Takes many sessions

WHAT DOESN'T WORK (BUT PEOPLE KEEP TRYING)

Just talking about it repeatedly without processing can actually re-traumatize.

Pushing through "Face your fears!" without nervous system support can make things worse.

Trying to "think differently" when the problem is in your body not your thoughts.

Ignoring it and hoping it goes away.

Spoiler: It won't.

WHEN TO SEEK PROFESSIONAL HELP

You should probably see a trauma therapist if you have: • Flashbacks (visual or emotional)

• Nightmares about the trauma • Avoiding places/people/situations that remind you • Hypervigilance (always scanning for danger)

• Startle easily • Can't feel positive emotions • Dissociation • Self-destructive behaviors • Can't maintain relationships • Chronic unexplained physical symptoms You deserve support. You don't have to do this alone. Find someone who specializes in trauma. Not just "general therapy"

Look for

EMDR certified

Somatic Experiencing trained

IFS trained

Trauma-informed Interview them, make sure you feel safe.

Because that IS the whole point.

SELF-CARE FOR TRAUMA RECOVERY

These won't cure trauma but they can support the healing.

Nervous system regulation (Everything in this book)

Movement (Especially shaking, yoga, walking)

Connection (With safe people)

Boundaries (Protecting your healing space)

Sleep (Non-negotiable)

Nutrition (Your brain needs fuel to heal)

Nature (Calms the nervous system)

Creativity (Expresses what words can't)

And time. Healing isn't linear.

You'll have good days and bad days.

That's normal. Stay with it.

POST-TRAUMATIC GROWTH: NOT JUST SURVIVAL

Here's something they don't tell you. Trauma can also lead to growth. Not "everything happens for a reason"

(That's toxic positivity)

But many people report their life became more meaningful after trauma and recovery.

Post-traumatic growth includes

Deeper relationships

Greater appreciation for life

Increased personal strength

New possibilities

Spiritual development

Research shows 50-90% of trauma survivors report at least one area of growth.

You don't have to be grateful for the trauma but you can acknowledge what you gained.

Through surviving and healing and learning.

I wouldn't wish my trauma on anyone.

But I wouldn't be who I am without it.

Both can be true.

THE NERVOUS SYSTEM REFRAME

Trauma symptoms aren't weakness but survival strategies that worked when you needed them.

Hypervigilance? Kept you safe when danger was real.

Dissociation? Let you escape when you couldn't physically.

People-pleasing? Reduced threat from unpredictable caregivers.

The problem isn't that you developed these strategies. The problem is they're still running and ruling even when the danger is gone.

Healing means thanking these parts for protecting you. Then gently updating them to let them know "The danger is over now"

"We're safe to relax now"

A LETTER TO YOUR TRAUMATIZED SELF

Dear [Your Name] I see you carrying all that weight, trying to look and act and seem normal, while your nervous system is screaming.

What happened to you wasn't your fault.

How you survived was brilliant.

Those coping mechanisms saved you then.

And now? You get to heal. Not "get over it"

Not "move on". But actually metabolize, process, integrate.

It won't be linear; it won't be quick But it is possible.

You don't have to carry this forever.

, Your Future Self , Next: The Daily Practice , building a life that supports your nervous system instead of hijacking it.

PAUSE & PRACTICE: Grounding in a Flashback If you're experiencing a flashback right now: 1. Name it "I'm having a flashback. This is from the past, not happening now."

2. Orient to present

Look around

Name 5 things you see 4 things you hear 3 things you can touch 3. Breathe 4-7-8 breathing Or just slow, deep breaths 4. Ground your body Feel your feet on floor

Press hands together

Splash cold water on face 5. Say out loud "I'm [name], I'm [age], I'm in [location], it's [date]"

"I'm safe right now"

This works. Keep practicing.

Your nervous system will learn

CHAPTER 13 , THE DAILY PRACTICE:

YOUR PERSONAL CALM PROTOCOL

Here's the problem with most self-help books.

You read them, feel inspired, do nothing and six months later?

You're exactly where you started This isn't that book.

Because by now you know: How your brain works. Why you react the way you do.

What trauma did to your wiring.

How to regulate your nervous system.

Now we build the practice. That makes it stick.

THE MINIMUM EFFECTIVE DOSE

You don't need two hours of self-care daily (Who has that much time to spare anyway?)

You need 15-30 minutes, strategically placed, consistently done.

Research shows that consistency beats intensity. Every. Single. Time.

15 minutes daily for 90 days beats 2 hours once a week.

Your nervous system needs regular input, not occasional overhauls.

THE MORNING PROTOCOL: SET YOUR NERVOUS SYSTEM

First hour of your day = Most important What you do in that hour determines your baseline state for the entire day.

THE DON'TS

Don't: Check your phone (seriously, not even once)

Check email/social media

Watch news

Start working

Respond to other people's needs first All of these put you in reactive mode from minute one. You don't need that.

THE DO'S (Pick 3-5)

Upon waking

Physiological sigh x3 (Before you even get out of bed)

Movement (5-10 minutes)

Stretching Yoga Walking Dancing to one song Whatever gets your body awake Breath practice (5 minutes)

Coherent breathing

Box breathing

Or just slow, deep breathing Gratitude (2 minutes)

Three specific things. Write or just think them.

Meditation (5-10 minutes) , Doesn't have to be fancy. Just sitting quietly following your breath works too.

Cold water (30 seconds)

Face splash or cold shower. Vagus nerve activation.

Sunlight (5-10 minutes)

Outside if possible. Sets circadian rhythm.

Nourishment Eat something preferably protein that stabilizes blood sugar.

Intention setting (1 minute)

"Today I'm practicing calm"

"Today I'm noticing beauty"

Whatever you need you give yourself.

THE MIDDAY RESET: WHEN YOUR NERVOUS SYSTEM GETS HIJACKED

Life happens. Stress accumulates. By noon you're already dysregulated. You need a midday reset.

SIGNS YOU NEED A RESET

• Tension in shoulders/jaw • Shallow breathing • Mind racing • Irritability • Fatigue • Can't focus • Snapping at people Don't wait until meltdown. Reset earlier.

THE 5-MINUTE MIDDAY PROTOCOL

1. Step away (literally)

Leave your desk/space Go outside if possible

Change your environment

2. Physiological sigh x 5 Resets your nervous system immediately 3. Move Walk. Shake. Stretch. Anything.

4. Hydrate You're probably dehydrated and that makes everything worse.

5. Ground Try the 5-4-3-2-1 technique 5 things you see 4 things you hear 3 things you touch 2 things you smell 1 thing you taste

, 6. One realistic affirmation "I'm handling this" OR "I can take one step"

OR, "I'm okay right now"

Do this 2-3 times daily before you crash. Not after.

THE EVENING WIND-DOWN: SIGNAL SAFETY

Your nervous system needs transition time.

From "switched on" to "rest"

Most people work until 6 pm. Scroll phone until 11 pm. Then wonder why they can't sleep.

That is because your body never got the signal that it's safe to rest.

THE 90-MINUTE WIND-DOWN

We covered this in the sleep chapter but it bears repeating.

90 minutes before desired sleep time: Turn off screens , (Yes, all of them)

Dim lights (Signals melatonin production)

Lower temperature (Your body needs to cool to sleep)

Transition activities Read (paper books).

Journal. Gentle stretching. Take a bath.

Meditate. Talk with loved ones (calmly)

30 minutes before bed:

Bedroom prep

Cool, dark, quiet. Phone in another room Anything you need for morning ready 15 minutes before bed: 4-7-8 breathing (4 cycles)

Body scan (progressive relaxation)

Gratitude (3 things from today)

Then: Lights out. Sleep.

THE WEEKLY PRACTICES

Some things need less frequency but still matter.

ONCE A WEEK

Movement that brings joy: Dance class.

Yoga. Hiking. Team sport. Whatever makes you forget you're "exercising"

Connection time: See friends. Call family.

Join a group. In person, when possible, not zoom or google meet.

Nature time: Minimum 2 hours in nature weekly. Park. Beach. Forest. Anywhere green/blue.

Review & plan: Look at your week. What worked? What didn't? Adjust accordingly.

ONCE A MONTH

Digital detox day

24 hours, no phone. We covered this.

It's non-negotiable.

Relationship audit

Who filled you up?

Who drained you?

Adjust accordingly

Trauma release

Longer movement practice. Somatic work.

Journaling. Therapy session. Whatever you need.

Something new

Try a new practice. Visit a new place. Learn something. Keeps neuroplasticity active

HABIT STACKING: MAKE IT EFFORTLESS

Don't rely on motivation. Build systems.

Habit stacking = Attach new habit to existing one.

Examples: After I pour my coffee, I do 5 minutes of stretching After I brush my teeth, I do 10 coherent breaths After I get in my car, I do 3 physiological sighs After I close my laptop, I write 3 gratitudes After I get in bed, I do 4-7-8 breathing The existing habit becomes the cue for the new one.

Research shows that habit stacking increases adherence by 47% compared to "I'll do it sometime today"

TRACKING: WHAT GETS MEASURED GETS MANAGED

You don't need an elaborate system.

Just awareness.

SIMPLE TRACKING

Daily: Mark an X on calendar for each practice you did.

Weekly: Rate your baseline calm (1-10)

Rate your sleep quality (1-10)

Rate your stress level (1-10)

Monthly: Look at patterns. Adjust practices Celebrate progress.

Use a simple notebook

Each day

✓ Morning practice ✓ Midday reset ✓ Evening wind-down Calm level: ____________________ That's it. Not complicated. Just consistent.

WHEN YOU FALL OFF TRACK

You will. Everyone does. Life happens: Travel. Illness. Family crisis. Work deadline.

Just... life The practice falls apart and that's normal

THE COMEBACK PROTOCOL

Don't restart everything at once. Pick ONE thing.

The non-negotiables

1. Morning breathing (5 min)

2. Evening wind-down (30 min)

3. One midday reset (5 min)

Start there. Rebuild from minimum. And forgive yourself. Seriously.

Self-punishment doesn't work – its counterproductive.

CUSTOMIZING YOUR PROTOCOL

My protocol isn't your protocol and that's okay.

Questions to ask yourself: What time of day do I have most energy?

(Do your practice then)

What practices actually feel good?

(Not what you "should" do, what you actually enjoy)

What's my biggest challenge?

(Sleep? Anxiety? Focus? Target that)

What's my schedule?

(Work with reality, not against it)

Who am I?

Morning person or night owl?

Extrovert or introvert?

Active or still?

Structured or flexible?

Build practices that fit YOU.

I'm a morning person so my practice is frontloaded and evening is minimal.

My friend is a night owl. Her main practice is 9 PM-10 pm so morning is just breathing Both work because they match our rhythms.

THE EMERGENCY PROTOCOL

For when everything is falling apart Panic attack incoming? Bad news just landed?

Triggered by something?

THE FAST RESET (2 minutes)

1. Physiological sigh x 5 Double inhale, long exhale Repeat 5 times 2. Cold water

Splash face

Or hold ice cube Activates mammalian dive reflex 3. Shake Literally shake your body 30 seconds

Discharge the activation

4. Name it "I'm having [anxiety/panic/flashback]"

"This is my nervous system"

"I'm safe right now"

5. Ground 5-4-3-2-1 Brings you to present This takes 2 minutes. Keep it on your phone.

Screenshot it

You'll forget when panicking

SEASONAL ADJUSTMENTS

Your needs change with seasons, with life phases, with stress levels.

Winter: More rest. More sleep. Gentler practices. Light therapy if needed.

Summer: More movement. More social.

Earlier wake times. Outdoor practices.

High-stress periods: More frequent resets.

Longer sleep. Simpler practices. More support Calm periods: Try new practices. Deepen existing ones. Maintain but don't force.

Listen to what you need.

Not what you "should" need.

THE 90-DAY TRANSFORMATION

Here's what happens when you actually do this for 90 days consistently.

Week 1-2: You feel awkward. It's hard to remember.

You skip days. That's normal Week 3-4: It's getting easier. You notice small shifts.

Sleep is better. Less reactive.

Week 5-8: It feels more natural. You miss it when you skip. Others notice you're calmer. You have more energy.

Week 9-12: It's automatic. Your baseline has shifted.

Old triggers don't hit as hard. You feel like a different person.

But actually? You're just more yourself.

The version anxiety was covering up.

THE RIPPLE EFFECT

Here's what nobody tells you. That when you regulate your nervous system everyone around you benefits.

Your kids Co-regulate with your calm Your partner Feels safer with you Your coworkers Feed off your stability Your friends Get the best version of you Calm is contagious. Just like anxiety is.

You're not just healing yourself.

You're changing the nervous system of everyone you touch.

THE LONG GAME

This isn't a 90-day fix. This is a life practice.

Some days will be easy. Some days will be hard. Some days you'll forget or give up entirely and that's okay. Just come back. The goal isn't perfection, it's a baseline shift From: Anxiety is my default To: Calm is my default From: I'm reactive To: I'm responsive From: I'm surviving To: I'm thriving Final chapter: Living as the new operating system, when calm becomes who you are, not what you do.

PAUSE & PRACTICE: Build Your Protocol Right now, create your minimum daily practice Morning: (Pick 3-5 things, 15-30 min total)

Midday: (5 min reset)

Evening: (30-60 min wind-down)

Write it down. Put it somewhere visible.

Tomorrow: Start.

No perfection required. Clumsily, scared lazily, however you wish to, start.

Just start.

Your nervous system is waiting to thank you.

CHAPTER 14 , LIVING AS THE NEW OPERATING SYSTEM: WHEN CALM BECOMES WHO YOU ARE

Six months from now someone will say to you "You seem different" And you will realize you are. Not because you became someone new, but because you finally became yourself.

Without all the static, without the worry, and with loving kindness to yourself.

THE IDENTITY SHIFT

There's a moment in healing where you stop thinking of yourself as broken. It's subtle. You don't announce it. You just... notice...

One day something stressful happens and you handle it. Calmly. Confidently.

Convincingly.

And you think "Huh. Old me would have spiraled."

That's the shift. From "I'm an anxious person trying to be calm" to "I'm a person who experiences anxiety sometimes"

From "I have PTSD" to: "I've experienced trauma and I'm healing"

From "I'm broken" to "I'm a work in progress"

The story changes. And so do you.

RECOGNIZING YOUR NEW BASELINE

How do you know it's working?

PHYSICAL SIGNS

Your body at rest

Jaw unclenched

Shoulders dropped

Breath deeper

Stomach settled

Sleep better
You don't feel constantly tired anymore. Not because you're doing less but because your nervous system isn't running at full throttle all day and every day.

EMOTIONAL SIGNS

Things that used to wreck you, now just...

don't That person who triggers you? Still annoying but you don't carry it for three days.

That worry that kept you up? Still there but it doesn't multiply into 47 scenarios You have space between stimulus and response.

Viktor Frankl said it perfectly: "Between stimulus and response there is a space. In that space is our power to choose our response. In our response lies our growth and our freedom."

You're living in that space now.

Congratulations

BEHAVIORAL SIGNS

You notice you're

Pausing before reacting

Setting boundaries without guilt Asking for what you need Saying no without over-explaining Letting things go faster Not ruminating for days Sleeping through the night

Actually enjoying things

The biggest one? You stop white-knuckling through life.

Old you: Tense, braced, waiting for disaster New you: Present, open, responsive.

WHEN OLD PATTERNS RESURFACE

They will, don't panic. Healing isn't linear, it's a spiral.

You'll circle back to old patterns, but at a higher level, with more awareness

The difference

Old you: Gets triggered, spirals for days, feels like all progress is lost New you: Gets triggered, notices quickly, uses tools, resets within hours , You still feel it. You just don't give it weight anymore.

Anxiety still shows up. Of course it will.

But now you say "Oh, hey. I see you. You're not real. You're just old wiring. I'm safe here.

You may go back to your jungle"

And it backs down. Faster every time.

THE MAINTENANCE PROTOCOL

You can't just "fix" your nervous system and forget about it like setting a broken bone and moving on.

This is more like physical fitness. You have to keep doing the work. For your mental fitness.

But here's the good news: Once it's your new normal it doesn't feel like work anymore.

THE MINIMUM TO MAINTAIN

Daily: Morning practice (15 min minimum)

One mindful pause during the day Evening wind-down (30 min minimum)

Weekly: One longer practice (movement, nature, connection)

Relationship check-ins

Adjustment as needed

Monthly:

Digital detox day

Review what's working

One session of deeper work (therapy, journaling, etc.)

That's it. To maintain a complete nervous system overhaul that's all it takes.

Worth it? Absolutely!

PROTECTING YOUR PROGRESS

As you heal, you'll need to protect your new baseline. This means:

CONTINUING TO SAY NO

To:

Toxic relationships

Energy vampires

Obligations that don't serve you People-pleasing Overcommitting Drama Your bandwidth has increased but that doesn't mean you fill it back with the same old chaos. Drop that I had to drop several friendships when I started healing. Not because they were bad people, but because their energy was incompatible with my new baseline.

It hurt but it was necessary.

CONTINUING TO PRIORITIZE YOUR PRACTICES

Life will always offer excuses: To skip your morning practice To stay up late scrolling To say yes when you mean no Don't let the world talk you out of what got you here. Your calm is not optional. It's foundational.

NAVIGATING STRESSFUL PERIODS WITHOUT UNRAVELING

Life will still happen: Deaths. Breakups.

Job loss. Health scares. Global pandemics (hope not, but apparently maybe)

The difference now? You don't add suffering to suffering.

Old pattern

Something bad happens

→ Spiral about how you can't handle it → Panic about panicking → Now you're dealing with the original thing → PLUS all the extra anxiety you added

New pattern

Something bad happens → "This is hard"

→ Use your tools → Ask for support → Feel your feelings → Keep showing up.

Pain is inevitable. Suffering is optional.

TEACHING OTHERS WHAT YOU'VE LEARNED

People will notice, and they will ask. "How are you so calm?" "What changed?"

"What are you doing differently?"

Here's what I've learned: Don't preach.

Nobody likes being evangelized to. If they ask specifically? Share one thing. The one thing that helped you most. Not everything at once.

And remember: Not everyone is ready and that's okay.

I spent years trying to "help" and "fix" my family members, forcing practices on them. It didn't work.

Now I just live differently, and some of them got curious and asked and...That's when change happens. When they're ready. Not when you are.

THE RIPPLE EFFECT (REVISITED)

Here's something beautiful that happens when you heal your nervous system.

You change your family's future.

Not just yours, Your children's, your grandchildren's. Because nervous system regulation is learned.

Children with regulated parents become regulated adults.

The trauma patterns that ran through your family for generations? They stop with you.

You became the circuit breaker.

A 2017 study on intergenerational trauma shows that parents who healed their own trauma had children with 60% less anxiety and 70% better emotional regulation.

You're not just healing yourself.

You're healing your lineage.

Past, present and future.

WHEN YOU BECOME THE CALM IN THE ROOM

There's a moment when you realize you are the one other people calm down around. You walk into a tense meeting and the energy shifts. Your friend is spiraling and your presence helps them ground.

Your kid is having a meltdown and your calm helps them regulate.

This is co-regulation in action. You are not trying to fix anyone. You're just being regulated and their nervous system picks up on it and they calm down too.

This is power. Not over people. But for people.

DEALING WITH PEOPLE WHO PREFERRED THE OLD YOU

This will happen and it will be uncomfortable.

Some people liked you anxious Because: You said yes to everything You didn't have boundaries You were easy to control You made them feel better about themselves You carried their emotions The new you will not do that. And they don't like it.

They might say

"You've changed" (accusatory)

"You're not fun anymore"

"You think you're better than us now"

"What's wrong with you?"

Translation: "I benefited from your dysfunction"

"And your healing threatens me"

Let them go. With compassion of course. But let them go. The right people will celebrate your healing.

REDEFINING SUCCESS

Old definition: Busy. Productive. Achieving.

Accumulating.

New definition: Regulated. Present.

Connected. Peaceful.

I used to measure success by how much I accomplished. Now? I measure it by how I feel at the end of the day.

Did I stay regulated?

Did I show up as myself?

Did I honor my needs?

Did I connect meaningfully?

That's success. Everything else is just stuff.

THE PARADOX OF HEALING

Here's something weird. The more you heal the less you need to talk about it.

Early healing

You want to tell everyone Process everything out loud

Analyze every insight

Later healing

You just... live it Quietly Solidly

Without announcement

You stop identifying as "healing." You are just... living. The work becomes invisible because it's integrated. Like breathing , You don't think about it, you just do it.

CELEBRATING THE SMALL WINS

Don't wait for complete transformation to acknowledge progress.

Celebrate: The first time you set a boundary without guilt The panic attack that only lasted 10 minutes instead of 2 hours The argument you didn't take personally The trigger you noticed before reacting The morning you woke up and felt... okay The full night's sleep The social event you actually enjoyed The decision you made from calm, not fear These are huge even though they may seem small.

I keep a "wins" journal. Just tiny moments where I showed up differently.

On hard days I read it and remember how far I've come.

WHEN YOU KNOW YOU'VE MADE IT

You don't wake up one day "healed" There is no finish line.

But there are markers. You know you've made it when: Old triggers still appear but they don't hook you „ You can be around chaos without absorbing it You trust yourself to handle whatever comes You say no without guilt You feel your feelings without being consumed by them You have space between what happens and how you respond You sleep well most nights You laugh easily and often You're not performing calm, you're experiencing it That's when you know.

A LETTER TO YOUR FUTURE SELF

Dear [Your Name] One year from now you're reading this

And smiling

Because you can barely remember what it felt like to be that anxious You still have hard days. But they are just days, not your entire existence You've learned that calm isn't the absence of chaos. It is the ability to be steady within it You've discovered that you are not broken.

Never were. You were just running outdated software on ancient hardware And now? You've updated. The upgrade took work. But it was worth every minute.

Because now you're living, not just surviving.

You are thriving.

Now you're present, not just getting through Now you're you. Fully, finally, beautifully YOU

Welcome home

, Your Past Self , (Who knew you could do this)

THE END IS THE BEGINNING

This is not the end of the book.

This is the beginning of your practice.

Everything you've read means nothing if you don't use it.

So, here's what you do next: Close this book. Take three slow breaths.

Feel your feet on the ground.

Then decide

Who do you want to be?

How do you want to feel?

What does your calm look like?

And start

Today. Right now. This moment.

Because your nervous system is always listening.

And it's ready for new instructions.

What will you tell it?

CALM SUTRA: THE FINAL PRACTICE

Sit comfortably. Close your eyes.

Place one hand on your heart.

Breathe in: "I am here"

Breathe out: “I am safe”

Breathe in: “I am learning”

Breathe out: “I am changing”

Breathe in: “I am enough”

Breathe out: “I am free”

Repeat as long as you need Then open your eyes

And live it

Welcome to your new operating system.

Where calm isn’t something you chase it's something you become.

Welcome to Calm Sutra.

The art and science of connection with yourself.

You’ve got this. You always did.

Now you know it. Go Enjoy it!

THE END

And the beginning...

CALM SUTRA - APPENDICES

APPENDIX A: QUICK REFERENCE GUIDE

, Emergency Protocols & Daily Practices IMMEDIATE STRESS RELIEF (Under 2 Minutes)

Physiological Sigh

Double inhale through nose Long exhale through mouth Repeat 1-3 times USE: Acute stress, panic, overwhelm

Cold Water on Face

Splash or immerse face for 15-30 seconds Activates mammalian dive reflex USE: Anxiety attacks, intense emotion

Shake It Off

Literally shake your whole body for 60 seconds

Discharges stress hormones

USE: After stressful events 5-4-3-2-1 Grounding: Name 5 things you see 4 things you hear 3 things you can touch 2 things you smell 1 thing you taste USE: Dissociation, panic, rumination

5-MINUTE PRACTICES

Box Breathing

Inhale 4, hold 4, exhale 4, hold 4 4-10 rounds USE: Before presentations, difficult conversations

Body Scan

Systematically relax from toes to head USE: Insomnia, chronic tension

Gratitude Practice

Write 3-5 specific things you're grateful for USE: Evening routine, shifting negative mood

Movement Snack

Stretch, shake, walk USE: Every hour while sitting

DAILY NON-NEGOTIABLES

Morning (15 min): 1. No phone first hour 2. Sunlight (10 min)

3. Movement (5 min)

4. Breathing (5 min)

Evening (20 min): 1. Digital sunset 90 min before bed 2. Gentle movement (15 min)

3. Journaling (5 min)

4. Breathing for sleep (5 min)

WEEKLY ESSENTIALS

• 1 restorative practice • 1 social connection • 1 play activity • 1 nature exposure • Review & adjust routine

SITUATION-SPECIFIC PROTOCOLS

Insomnia: 1. 4-7-8 breathing 2. Body scan 3. Cognitive shuffle 4. If awake 20+ min, leave room briefly

Anxiety Attack

1. Cold water on face 2. Physiological sighs 3. 5-4-3-2-1 grounding 4. Name it: "This is anxiety. It will pass."

Anger: 1. Physical discharge (safe hitting, pushing wall, shaking)

2. Alternate nostril breathing 3. Walk or vigorous movement 4. Journal the anger out Depression/Shutdown: 1. Cold exposure (shower)

2. Vigorous movement 3. Sunlight 4. Social connection (text/call someone)

5. Upbeat music Overwhelm: 1. Brain dump (write everything down)

2. Box breathing 3. One thing at a time (literally say "one thing")

4. Movement break

APPENDIX B: RESOURCES

BOOKS

Neuroscience & Trauma: The Body Keeps the Score , Bessel van der Kolk Why We Sleep , Matthew Walker The Polyvagal Theory , Stephen Porges My Stroke of Insight , Jill Bolte Taylor Why Zebras Don't Get Ulcers , Robert Sapolsky Breath & Movement: Breath: The New Science of a Lost Art ,

James Nestor

The Oxygen Advantage , Patrick McKeown Waking the Tiger , Peter Levine Mindset & Language: Atomic Habits , James Clear Mindset , Carol Dweck Self-Compassion , Kristin Neff

Digital Wellness

Digital Minimalism , Cal Newport How to Break Up With Your Phone ,

Catherine Price

APPS & TOOLS

Breathing: Breathwrk

Prana Breath

Box Breathing (simple, free)

Meditation: Insight Timer (free with premium option)

Waking Up , Sam Harris

Ten Percent Happier

Sleep:

Sleep Cycle

Rise (sleep debt tracker)

Oura Ring or WHOOP (HRV tracking)

Digital Detox

Freedom (app/website blocker)

Opal (screen time management)

Forest (gamified focus)

One Sec (pause before opening apps)

Journaling: Day One (digital journal)

Physical notebooks work best for many Movement: Down Dog (yoga, customizable)

Peloton (if you have equipment)

YouTube (free yoga, tai chi, HIIT)

FINDING PRACTITIONERS

Somatic Therapists

Somatic Experiencing: traumahealing.org

Sensorimotor Psychotherapy

sensorimotorpsychotherapy.org EMDR: emdria.org (find certified practitioners)

Nervous System Support

Polyvagal-informed therapists

Body-based psychotherapists

Integrative/functional medicine doctors

What to Look For

Trauma-informed

Body-based approaches

Good fit (trust your gut)

Credentials verified

Red Flags

Promises quick fixes

Dismisses medication if needed Makes you feel worse consistently

Boundary violations

ONLINE COMMUNITIES

Reddit: r/Anxiety r/CPTSD r/Meditation r/DecidingToBeBetter Note: Be discerning. Take what helps, leave what doesn't.

RESEARCH DATABASES

For those who want to dive deeper: PubMed (medical research)

Google Scholar

ResearchGate Huberman Lab Podcast (neuroscience translation)

APPENDIX C: THE SCIENCE

BIBLIOGRAPHY

Key Studies Cited by Chapter

CHAPTER 1:

King's College London (2018) , Childhood trauma and amygdala changes Stanford (2018) , Neuroplasticity across lifespan Harvard (2019) , Childhood neglect and hippocampus size LeDoux, J. (1996) , Amygdala and fear processing Sapolsky, R. (2004) , Why Zebras Don't Get Ulcers

CHAPTER 2:

MacLean, P. (1990) , Triune brain model MIT (2016) , Threat response timing Schore, A. (2001) , Affect regulation and attachment UC Berkeley (2020) , 30-day mindfulness study Siegel, D. (2010) , Prefrontal cortex functions

CHAPTER 3:

Merzenich, M. (1983) , Adult brain plasticity Maguire, E. (2000) , London taxi driver hippocampal changes Harvard (2014) , Juggling and gray matter Boyd, L. (2015) , Practice frequency vs. intensity Frontiers in Human Neuroscience (2018) , Timeline of neuroplastic change

CHAPTER 4:

Pert, C. (1997) , Molecules of Emotion University of California (2018) , Chronic cortisol effects Stanford (2019) , Social media dopamine spikes JAMA Psychiatry (2019) , Nature and serotonin Carnegie Mellon (2019) , Stress and inflammation UCLA (2013) , Meditation and gene expression

CHAPTER 5:

Porges, S. (2011) , Polyvagal Theory UNC (2010) , Vagal tone and health outcomes Stanford (2022) , Physiological sigh study

European Journal of Applied Physiology

(2014) , Cold exposure Multiple studies on vagal activation techniques

CHAPTER 6:

Walker, M. (2017) , Why We Sleep Nedergaard, M. (2012) , Glymphatic system discovery Boston University (2019) , Real-time glymphatic imaging UC Berkeley (2018) , Sleep deprivation and amygdala Harvard (2015) , Blue light and sleep

CHAPTER 7:

Bohr, C. (1904) , Bohr effect (CO2 and oxygen release)

Stanford (2017) , Breathing and cortisol reduction Military study (2019) , Box breathing efficacy University of Pisa (2018) , Chest breathing and anxiety Weil, A. (2018) , 4-7-8 breathing validation

CHAPTER 8:

van der Kolk, B. (2014) , The Body Keeps the Score Levine, P. (1997) , Somatic Experiencing theory University of Maryland (2017) , Exercise and cortisol Cell Metabolism (2019) , Exercise and

BDNF

Journal of Bodywork and Movement

Therapies (2017) , Myofascial release

CHAPTER 9:

Carnegie Mellon (2016) , Self-talk and brain activation Cognitive Processing (2017) , Positive framing University of Pennsylvania (2014) ,

Effective affirmations

Pennebaker, J. (multiple studies) ,

Expressive writing

Emmons, R. (2003) , Gratitude journaling

CHAPTER 10:

University of California (2019) , Phone use statistics Kross, E. (University of Michigan) , Social media and well-being Harris, T. (2019) , Digital attention economy Multiple studies on social media detox effects

CHAPTER 11:

Porges, S. , Co-regulation research Multiple attachment theory studies 2018 study , Safe relationships and vagal tone

CHAPTER 12:

van der Kolk, B. , Trauma and the body Siegel, D. , Window of tolerance EMDR research (multiple studies)

Post-traumatic growth literature

Major Researchers Referenced

Neuroscience: Dr. Andrew Huberman (Stanford)

Dr. Matthew Walker (UC Berkeley)

Dr. Robert Sapolsky (Stanford)

Dr. Joseph LeDoux (NYU)

Dr. Bessel van der Kolk (Trauma Center)

Neuroplasticity: Dr. Michael Merzenich (UC San Francisco)

Dr. Lara Boyd (UBC)

Dr. Eleanor Maguire (University College London)

Polyvagal Theory & Nervous System: Dr. Stephen Porges (Indiana University)

Dr. Peter Levine (Somatic Experiencing)

Dr. Deb Dana (Polyvagal application)

Psychology & Mindset: Dr. Carol Dweck (Stanford)

Dr. Kristin Neff (UT Austin)

Dr. James Pennebaker (UT Austin)

Dr. Daniel Siegel (UCLA)

Breathing: Dr. Andrew Weil

James Nestor

Patrick McKeown

How to Stay Updated

Podcasts: Huberman Lab (neuroscience)

On Being (spirituality meets science)

The Tim Ferriss Show (optimization)

Hidden Brain (psychology)

Newsletters:

Huberman Lab newsletter

Peter Attia MD (health)

James Clear (habits)

Following Research

Set up Google Scholar alerts for topics you're interested in Follow researchers on social media Read systematic reviews and meta-analyses

Important Note on Research

Science evolves

What's true today may be refined tomorrow

Hold insights loosely

But practice consistently

The fundamentals won't change: Your breath affects your state Your body holds stress Your brain can rewire

Connection matters

Movement helps

Sleep is essential

Trust the principles.

Adjust the practices as science advances.

FINAL NOTE: YOUR JOURNEY CONTINUES

This is a beginning.

Not an ending.

You now have

Understanding of your nervous system Knowledge of what calm actually is Tools to regulate yourself Practices to build on Science to back it all up What you do with it is up to you Remember:

Progress over perfection

Consistency over intensity

Compassion over criticism

Practice over knowledge

The work is simple. But not easy.

It requires

Showing up

Trying again when you fail Being gentle with yourself

Trusting the process

And it's worth it. Because the alternative?

Living in chronic dysregulation is no way to live.

You deserve calm

You deserve peace

You deserve to feel safe in your own body and mind And now you know how to get there Go practice. Your nervous system is waiting.

With gratitude and hope for your healing, , T-Light

Printed at Repro India Ltd.